A superb—and superbly readable—analysis of the way our ruling elites manufacture their own legitimacy and protect wealth and power. While deploring the rise of authoritarian nationalist movements of the Right, the authors do not shy away from criticizing the Left's focus on identity politics of race and gender which has diverted attention from the fundamental requirement to tackle the injustices and irrationality caused by capitalism. Yet Derber and Magrass offer hope as they outline the growing moves by progressive Americans to build united fronts at the local and state level which are challenging the dominant narrative and bringing significant social and economic change and genuine security. Derber and Magrass provide a much-needed and optimistic antidote to Trump-inspired gloom.

Jonathan Steele, former Chief Foreign Correspondent for *The Guardian*

I love how *Moving Beyond Fear* weaves the metaphor of the upstairs/downstairs house throughout the book to paint an easy-to-understand picture of a capitalist-built house where the wealth produced by downstairs workers goes to a few upstairs residents living in luxury. Derber and Magrass show how the mortar holding this wobbly house together is fear and insecurity, and how the weaknesses of the left have failed to shake its foundation. Their solution? Read the book. A much more beautiful home in which we all thrive is awaiting.

Medea Benjamin, founder of CODEPINK; author of *Inside Iran*

I just devoured this book. It's hard to put down once you start it. *Moving Beyond Fear* exposes the playbook of authoritarian leaders, past and present. As the American Dream fades, political leaders use fear, fostering "security stories" to turn the lower classes against one another. This is a must-read for those eager to stem fascism and the looming catastrophes of climate change and nuclear proliferation.

Kathleen Odell Korgen, William Paterson University; author of *The Engaged Sociologist*

This book is just what's needed. It explains lucidly and powerfully how fear is used from anti-immigrant nationalist politics throughout history into the Trump White House and right-wing radio today. Derber and Magrass give us the analytical tools to understand the power of "security stories" and their role in legitimating the interests of authoritarian elites. *Moving Beyond Fear* is an engaging read to help us reject the politics and narratives of fear for an authentic security of greater equity, social injustice, and vibrant democracy.

Chuck Collins, Institute for Policy Studies; author of *Born on Third Base*

Derber and Magrass offer a timely critique of US national security policy. They show how successive US administrations have created false enemies to justify expansion of empire. They criticize both right-wing Republicans and the liberal Democrats who have failed to provide effective opposition. Their book is essential reading for anyone interested in national security issues.

Reese Erlich, freelance foreign correspondent for NPR, CBC, and Foreign Policy; author of *The Iran Agenda Today, Inside Syria,* and *Conversations with Terrorists*

Why do people vote against their best interests? Why do many working people vote for their class enemy, a con artist who is dedicated slavishly to wealth and private power and is shafting them at every turn? The question is carefully addressed in this powerful study which explores a central part of the answer: the "security story" mixed with "raw tribalism," an amalgam with ancient vintage, commonly implemented in ways that gravely undermine security. Not for the first time in history—and as Mark Twain reminded us, while history doesn't repeat, it rhymes. Sometimes ominously, sometimes with hope.

Noam Chomsky

Moving Beyond Fear

While security stories often point to real threats, the narratives of leaders are as much about legitimating the power of rulers and the political and economic system that brought them to power. Derber and Magrass offer a penetrating examination of this phenomenon across history and types of societies. Their analysis reveals the great irony about security stories: *they historically increase insecurity, imperiling citizens and nation.* In the US today, the contradiction is especially acute, as security stories told by Trump divide US citizens against one another.

The book builds from an analysis of the extreme dangers of the prevailing security stories to a new paradigm of true security. The authors develop new approaches as our best hope for avoiding catastrophe and creating a socially just society based on real security for a nation and for humans across the planet.

Charles Derber is Professor of Sociology at Boston College. An internationally renowned scholar and public intellectual, he has written 21 books, translated into eight languages, and more than 100 articles, including op-eds for the *New York Times, Boston Globe, Newsday, Truthout,* and others. He appears frequently on national television and on radio programs, and is featured on hundreds of YouTube channels and other online sites.

Yale R. Magrass is Chancellor Professor of Sociology/Anthropology at the University of Massachusetts—Dartmouth. He is the author of six books and over 60 articles, and frequently makes public appearances and presentations.

Universalizing Resistance Series
Edited by Charles Derber and Suren Moodliar

Welcome to the Revolution
Universalizing Resistance for Social Democracy
in Perilous Times (2017)
Charles Derber

Moving Beyond Fear
Upending the Security Tales in Capitalism, Fascism,
and Democracy (2019)
Charles Derber and Yale R. Magrass

Forthcoming:

Disrupting Narratives of Deservedness
Changing the Stories that Hold Economic and
Racial Inequality in Place (2020)
Chuck Collins

¡Viva Latinx!
How a New Generation of Organized Power Can
Win Elections and Transform Culture (2020)
Elisa Batista and Matt Nelson

For more information about this series, please visit:
www.routledge.com/Universalizing-Resistance/book-series/RESIST

Moving Beyond Fear

Upending the Security Tales in
Capitalism, Fascism, and Democracy

Charles Derber and Yale R. Magrass

Routledge
Taylor & Francis Group

NEW YORK AND LONDON

First published 2019
by Routledge
52 Vanderbilt Avenue, New York, NY 10017

and by Routledge
2 Park Square, Milton Park, Abingdon, Oxon, OX14 4RN

Routledge is an imprint of the Taylor & Francis Group, an informa business

© 2019 Taylor & Francis

The right of Charles Derber and Yale R. Magrass to be identified as authors of this work has been asserted by them in accordance with sections 77 and 78 of the Copyright, Designs and Patents Act 1988.

Library of Congress Cataloging-in-Publication Data
A catalog record for this book has been requested

ISBN: 978-1-138-65667-3 (hbk)
ISBN: 978-1-138-65668-0 (pbk)
ISBN: 978-1-315-62177-7 (ebk)

Typeset in Adobe Caslon Pro
by Apex CoVantage, LLC

CONTENTS

INTRODUCTION

THE SECURITY STORY: WHY IT ENDANGERS EVERYTHING AND HOW TO RESIST IT

Do you realize that in addition to fluoridating water, why, there are studies underway to fluoridate salt, flour, fruit juices, soup, sugar, milk, ice cream? Ice cream, Mandrake? Children's ice cream! . . . You know when fluoridation began? . . . 1946. 1946, Mandrake. How does that coincide with your post-war Commie conspiracy, huh? It's incredibly obvious, isn't it? A foreign substance is introduced into our precious bodily fluids without the knowledge of the individual, and certainly without any choice. That's the way your hard-core Commie works. I first became aware of it, Mandrake, during the physical act of love. . . . Yes, a profound sense of fatigue, a feeling of emptiness followed. Luckily I. . . . I was able to interpret these feelings correctly. Loss of essence. I can assure you it has not recurred, Mandrake. Women, er, women sense my power, and they seek the life essence. I do not avoid women, Mandrake . . . but I do deny them my essence. . . .

I can no longer sit back and allow Communist infiltration, Communist indoctrination, Communist subversion, and the international Communist conspiracy to sap and impurify all of our precious bodily fluids.

—Base Commander General Jack D. Ripper
(Sterling Hayden) in the 1964 movie *Dr. Strangelove*

To preserve our precious bodily fluids, General Ripper launched a unilateral full-scale nuclear attack upon the Soviet Union.

This is a book about an ancient Security story. It has been a dominant story in societies for a very long time. It is a narrative about a dangerous world and how people can protect themselves from all sorts of threats in order to live a good life. Humans need to feel secure and the Security story is the narrative created by rulers that promises to provide the true security that their people crave.

Leaders in different societies craft and spread their own versions of the Security story. In the US, we have what amounts to a religion of national security that trumps almost every other doctrine in our society. The Security establishment—in America rooted in the military and its many security agencies—is sacred. Those who fight to protect us are considered heroes, a common moral theme in many modern nations. But the military is only one part of our Security story, since the story tells us how to confront domestic enemies that can't be defeated only by war but also by economic and political strategies devised by the rulers.

In every society, the Security story is different. But they all seek to reassure the population about how they can be protected by the rulers themselves and the society or nation that the elites have constructed. The Security story is not just a narrow tale about safety but an overarching justification for the legitimacy of the rulers and of the economic, political and military institutions they govern.

Security stories in all societies are ruling ideologies. Security is a foundation of all societies, and a society without a credible Security story will be imperiled. Moreover, security is such a basic need that Security stories tend to be a dominant part of the culture. The Security story is a window into the soul of a nation or society and reveals many secrets about its rulers.

At the heart of all Security stories is a focus on enemies that endanger the people and the nation. Security stories are tales about a frightening world and the many threats that rulers tell us need to be taken very seriously. These threats come from enemies outside the nation but they also include frightening enemies living in the nation. The Security story headlines both the foreign and domestic enemies, and it tells people how their rulers will protect them from both.

The great irony about Security stories is that they historically increase insecurity. Both individuals and the nation are usually imperiled by their own Security tales. In the US, this contradiction is particularly acute. In the name of saving us from enemies, it creates a world full of ever more frightening enemies that hate us. In the name of protecting us from danger, it creates an ever more dangerous world. In the name of securing the nation, it divides people living within it as enemies of each other, increasing hatred and distrust within our borders as well as outside them.

In the American case, the Security story takes this contradiction beyond any apparent sanity. For in the name of providing security, the Security story and the rulers who carry out its policies are creating and intensifying the most extreme dangers humanity has faced. As long as the Security story—and the institutions and policies organized in its name—is carried out, the greater the chance that humanity itself will not survive. Moreover, the story enshrines institutions and cultural norms that degrade the economic and social well-being of the people, as well as the feelings of solidarity that can create peace across the world and within the nation itself.

In the US today, the Security story is threatening the very survival of our democracy. In the name of security, leaders and governing parties are tightening forms of political and military control over popular expression, free speech and all kinds of protests on the streets. Authoritarianism in the name of security is now one of the greatest dangers posed by a story intended to protect us from danger.

How is it possible that a Security story can create more insecurity and fuel unprecedented dangers? How can such a contradictory narrative be embraced by both rulers and a significant percentage of the people who follow them? This seems like madness—and it is the great paradox that we explore here. It is only by explaining the origins of the story and how it gains emotional public resonance that we can discredit the story and create the true security that all humans deserve.

We show here that the Security story is not typically crafted by leaders to create security, especially in societies that are unequal and unjust. Instead, leaders spin these tales to justify their own rule and the system that has brought them to power. In other words, the Security story is one of the most common forms of what the Italian philosopher, Antonio Gramsci, called a "legitimation" doctrine. Such a story is all about legitimating or justifying the power of rulers. It preserves their own power and the political and economic system that they design and run. The need for and importance of such legitimating stories increase as inequality and injustice grow—and threaten the stability of the system and the power of the leaders.

In the United States, we have a capitalist society that has increasingly deep divisions between the wealthy and the rest of the society. It is a capitalist democracy, but as economic inequality increases—and the wealth at the top becomes as large as $107 billion dollars owned by one person, Jeff Bezos, CEO of Amazon and the richest man in the world, while more than about half of Americans have no wealth at all—it is not hard to explain why our economic order may need a more compelling legitimating story. When our leaders are billionaires, such as Donald Trump, and most political leaders in both mainstream parties are very rich and serve the even wealthier donors who pay for their campaigns, faith in the system and its rulers weakens. When legitimating ideas about the ability of everyone to work hard and become successful are thrown into doubt, legitimating stories of capitalist democracy must adapt and persuade ordinary people that their society remains both democratic and just.

This is the context for understanding the rise of the Security story in the United States. US elites are ruling a society that is not fulfilling its economic or democratic promises. This is happening in a period of great demographic change, new immigration and cultural ferment increasing feelings of both economic and cultural anxiety in much of the population. This is a textbook case for the rise of legitimating stories that are deeply irrational, as in the cases of the Security story that increases insecurity.

The Security story now ruling in the US has very ancient roots. American rulers have reached back to the Middle Ages and before, where people faced all kind of threats—including the tyranny of the societies and kings that ruled them—that generated their own legitimating stories around security. Our Security story today has a modern 21st-century dress, but its roots and purposes go back deep into human history, perhaps as far back as any legitimating story.

We are playing out a modern and especially dangerous version of this ancient story. Despite great technological, material and social progress, and the rise of modern democracies, we live in profit-driven and militarized nations that inflict suffering on much of the population and are now leading to the greatest threats ever faced related to survival of human civilization. The problem with the Security story is not the absence of a security threat—in fact, never has there been a period of such danger to the planet. It is rather that the Security story is inventing false threats, worsening real threats and making it harder to stop them from destroying much that we hold sacred. The greatest threat of all is the militaristic capitalist elite itself who use the security story to rally the 99% to forget their real needs and instead willingly maintain their rulers' profit and power.

Our aim, then, is to show how the Security story has been designed, what its true aims are and why it is the most dangerous story ever told. We explain how the ancient Security story resurrected today could move us from capitalist democracy to capitalist authoritarianism or even fascism.

We conclude by offering suggestions about how to discredit such an insane Security story and create a new narrative and social system that can actually offer the authentic security—and nurture democracy and social justice—that humans deserve and need. The book builds from an analysis of the extreme dangers of the reigning Security stories to a new paradigm of true security. In the last chapter, we flesh out the new paradigm as our best hope for avoiding catastrophe and creating a socially just society based on safety derived from universal rights and international collective security. This, it turns out, is the highest priority both for progressives and for humans across the planet.

1

THE UPSTAIRS/
DOWNSTAIRS HOUSE

SELLING CAPITALISM IN AN
AGE OF EXTREME INEQUALITY

Inequality is as dear to the American heart as Liberty itself.
—William Dean Howells

Girls: Free to be anything you choose
Boys: Free to wait tables and shine shoes
—Verse from the song, "America," *West Side Story*

We googled "inequality" in May 2018, and found over 85 million search items. Now, admittedly, that is only about half of the number of searches for the pop icon, Lady Gaga. But you won't find many words that generate almost 100 million search items. It's a sign that inequality, if not exactly as popular as pop culture, interests almost everyone who thinks about society—and has economic, political, social, military, cultural and psychological effects on all of us, rich or poor. As inequality has become more extreme, and because it is rooted in the DNA of our economies and societies, more and more people realize we may have to rethink such notions as capitalism and the American Dream, because they can morph into something darker and scarier.

Economist Thomas Piketty, the leading global scholar on inequality, offers a very simple explanation for why 85 million people might google inequality. The inequality gap has become unbelievably extreme, in the US and the entire world. Piketty, a sober, data-driven academic, who has collected more data than anyone else on inequality, says this:

> Income from labor [in the United States] is about as unequally distributed as has ever been observed anywhere.[1]

In other words, we live in a society where income inequality is greater than ever before experienced in human history.

Consider a few more of the most striking illustrations of our extreme and deepening inequality in the US house:

- In 2017, three white men in the US owned as much wealth as the bottom half of the population or 160 million people.[2]
- In 2014, the top .1% owned as much wealth as the bottom 90%.[3]
- In 2014, 30% of US households had zero or negative wealth.[4]
- Income inequality is higher in the US than in any other developed nation—with a Gini coefficient (a measure of inequality) of .40.[5]
- The top 10% of US families own $51 trillion in wealth or about 75% of total household US wealth.[6]
- According to Thomas Piketty, the bottom half of the US population owns just 2% of the nation's wealth.[7]
- Based on IRS figures, summarized by University of California economists, 95% of the income gains reported in the US from 2009 to 2013 went to the top 1%, a pattern consistent during recent decades of the wealthiest Americans capturing almost all the growth in the nation's income and capital stock.[8]
- According to empirical data collected by the Institute for Policy Studies and the Poor People's campaign, 140 million Americans in 2017 are poor or low-income, living in the basement or the decaying first floor rooms of the downstairs.

Of course, our society is a capitalist one—and it's not entirely surprising to find that inequality is a big deal in capitalism. If we think of capitalist societies as houses, what would they look like? All of them would be "upstairs-downstairs" structures, though the floors and staircases would differ in their design. If we looked at the world as a global capitalist system, we would see a huge neighborhood of different styles of homes, but all of them would be some version of upstairs-downstairs architecture, reflecting structural inequality in the capitalist DNA.

Upstairs-downstairs will remind many of *Downton Abbey*, the PBS television hit series about the British aristocracy and their servants. It followed an earlier BBC series, *Upstairs Downstairs*. It was even more popular than *Downton Abbey*, with seven Emmys and viewed by an average of 9 million people each episode, and a billion people worldwide.[9] In both shows, the aristocracy and servants occupied two interdependent worlds—of luxury and power upstairs and indentured servitude downstairs. The shows describe the economically and emotionally inter-tangled lives both within and across the upstairs and downstairs in a late 19th-century Gilded Age of lords and servants, a residue of feudalism in capitalist Britain during the two World Wars.

When a noble lady in the series *Upstairs Downstairs* once gets into the front seat of her chauffeur's car, he asks her to go back because she and he must abide by the rules. "Their relationship is where the two sides—upstairs and downstairs—meet," the actor playing the chauffeur told a journalist.

> She shuns the archetype of who she's supposed to be, and he shuns having to bow down to authority.[10]

This is extremely upsetting and dangerous. Authority is everything. Those upstairs and downstairs know the rules well and violate them at their risk.

The upstairs/downstairs double worlds have not gone away—they just seem to be less rigid and more democratic today, disguising the persisting enormous chasms in wealth and power. Many of us think we have moved beyond such fossilized class-bound worlds. But despite economic growth spurred by new technology and progressive reforms, *Upstairs Downstairs* and *Downton Abbey* became huge hits partly because they shocked us with a certain unexpected familiarity, giving us a sub-conscious recognition of how little has changed. As one reviewer says of Sarah, a maid in the *Upstairs Downstairs* series:

> Like us (the TV audience), she's forced to accept stark social divisions in the same house as perfectly normal.[11]

In other words, the billion viewers of the show see how our current world takes for granted its own upstairs/downstairs reality, and "normalizes" and perpetuates ancient patterns of inequality and injustice, in new modern dress.

Critics and backers of capitalism both see that the upstairs/downstairs great divides are wired into the capitalism order. The greatest critic, Karl Marx, argued that capitalism is a permanent upstairs/downstairs system in which the upstairs capitalist class—the owners of factories, banks and other "means of production"—squeeze profit from the vast, exploited working class on the first floor. Anti-Marxist champions of capitalism—from Adam Smith to Milton Friedman, from Teddy Roosevelt to George W. Bush—strongly agree with Marx on one thing: inequality is baked into the system. But they view the house as beautifully designed, with the upstairs/downstairs architecture essential for prosperity, freedom and justice, since it allows the most productive and worthy people—the "creatives" as novelist and capitalist champion Ayn Rand put it—to move up the staircases based on their merit and hard work, while the lazy "parasites," Rand's term for the rest of the population, get their just retribution in the drab first floor or dirty basement. Here is Rand unabashed on why the "creatives" belong upstairs and the "parasites" downstairs:

> The creator stands on his own judgment. The parasite follows the opinions of others. The creator thinks, the parasite copies. The creator produces, the parasite loots.[12]

What does the US capitalist house look like? It has a lavish upstairs, where Donald Trump, Steve Forbes, Charles and David Koch, Jeff Bezos and all the other "creative" capitalists—now dubbed the 1%—live luxuriously and can push buttons that control the societal house. The top .01%—16,000 households led by CEOs, hedge fund managers and multi-millionaires with minimum wealth over $100 million—are the true capitalist aristocrats living at the very top of the house, led in 2018 by over 400 billionaires.[13] They fund both our political parties, and pass their riches on to their heirs—in what Piketty calls "patrimonial capitalism" where inherited wealth exceeds earned wealth. These "aristocratic capitalists" thereby inherit the keys to running America.

Inequality analyst Chuck Collins writes that we have very ambivalent views of the upstairs rich:

> At one talk I gave, I asked the audience "How many of you feel rage toward the wealthiest 1%?" Almost everyone in a room of 350 people raised a hand. There was nervous laughter.
>
> "How many of you have admiration for some of things wealthy people have to done to make our society better?"
>
> About two-thirds of the people raised their hands.
>
> "How many of you wish you were in the wealthiest 1%?"
>
> Again, almost everyone raised a hand, laughing.
>
> "So you feel enraged, admiring and wish to be the object of your own anger?" I observed. See, I told you it was complicated.[14]

But our mixed-up feelings—and our partial beliefs in Ayn Rand's ideas—shouldn't obscure the stark realities of the house architecture. Beneath the opulent quarters of the multi-millionaires, the house has a huge downstairs, with many different rooms and partitions on the first floor, where the working class (which includes blue-collar, pink-collar and white-collar employees comprising perhaps 70% of Americans) lives under a wide degree of economically insecure, indebted and declining conditions. Nearly half of all Americans, or 155 million people, lived within 200% of the official poverty line in 2011, which many economists define as the most accurate measure of poverty. Many of these people live in the downstairs basement but a much higher percentage live on the first floor and are mis-named middle class.[15]

The house also has a fashionable mezzanine, closer to the upstairs than the downstairs, inhabited by the generally well-off and culturally authoritative professional-managerial class (the PMC), a group of highly educated doctors, lawyers, professors, journalists and other professional or managerial employees numbering perhaps 10% of the population, dubbed the "new class" by the sociologist Alvin Gouldner.[16] It has more wealth than the top .1% and the entire downstairs combined. If, in 2016, you were a typical working person in the bottom 90% in wealth, you would have to increase that wealth twelvefold (good luck with that!) to leapfrog on to the PMC mezzanine.[17]

The PMC has great authority as well as wealth and is increasingly recognized as its own kind of "aristocracy," perpetuating itself through inbreeding, professional educational credentialing and residential segregation. The PMC is very important in our story; the different sectors of PMC help administer the house but in ways that both reinforce and challenge the capitalist elite above it upstairs, while also contradictorily helping and disrespecting the less-educated and much poorer people downstairs.

Journalist Matthew Stewart, a member in good standing of the PMC, says this about his class:

> So what kind of characters are we. . . .? We are mostly not like those flamboyant political manipulators from the .1 percent. We're a well-behaved, flannel-suited crowd of lawyers, doctors, dentists, mid-level investment banks, MBAs with opaque job titles and associated other professionals—the kind of people you might invite to dinner. In fact we're so self-effacing, we deny our own existence. We keep insisting that we're "middle class."
>
> As of 2016, it took $1.2 million in net worth to make it into (our class) . . . our necks get stuck in the upward position. We gaze upon the .1% with a mixture of awe, envy and eagerness to obey. As a consequence, we are missing the other big story of our time. We have left the 90 percent in the dust—and we've been quietly tossing down roadblocks behind us to make sure they never catch up.[18]

Those who almost never catch up live in a dark dirt-floor basement, where millions of unemployed and poor people have a miserable life, often hungry and sick. They are disproportionately people of color and undocumented immigrants, though the majority in the basement are native whites and rural. About 16% or about 55 million Americans are officially poor. Almost half of the nation (155 million people)—and 41% of US children in 2016 live "on the brink of poverty," translating into 29.8 million children and 5 million toddlers under the age of three.[19]

The other key to the capitalist architecture is the much celebrated staircases, permitting people to move up and live the American Dream (but also to fall down). There is a long, winding staircase connecting the upstairs to the downstairs. The image of Donald Trump coming down the brilliantly lit gilded staircase (actually an escalator, symbolically suggesting the stairwell will move you up effortlessly) in Trump Tower when he announced his presidential candidacy is a perfect image for the house. The "people's billionaire" inspires everyone with the grandeur of the house and how we can all dream of being him—because America is built around huge staircases of mobility that make everyone's American Dream possible.

There are many staircases in the house. One connects the mezzanine to the upstairs, and another staircase goes from the first floor to the mezzanine, and both seem possible to climb but are, as we soon see, very steep climbs, something like going up Mt. Everest. And then there is a chute where people from the downstairs can fall down into the basement, but the Happy House tells us that those not lazy can easily climb out of the basement.

In any upstairs/downstairs societal architecture, the house needs a seductive and moralistic governing creed—or set of creeds—to survive. The folks upstairs—think Donald Trump or Jeff Bezos or the wealthiest people in your favorite big city—just live too much better and enjoy far more power than those stagnating downstairs despite working harder than ever. The cultural authority of the PMC on the mezzanine—helping define the good life for the working people downstairs—also creates a huge division, in which workers downstairs feel put down by the arrogance and cultural authority of the PMC. An architecture built to sustain such deep capitalist-driven economic inequality and PMC-driven cultural inequality can make anyone ask the big question: why such vast divisions should be allowed to persist or exist at all?

If no good, persuasive answers are presented, a huge crisis of faith in the system—what the Italian theorist, Antonio Gramsci, calls a "legitimation crisis"—can explode anytime.[20] Suppose that all Americans knew that Trump was born upstairs to a very rich New York real estate father, Philip Trump, a mafia-style racist realtor who bequeathed him at least $40 million—the exact number is disputed though the father's total estate was about $300 million.[21] Donald might be even richer today if he had simply put his inheritance in the bank, saved the interest, and not worked at all. That might raise some eyebrows and stir uncomfortable discontent among millions of those who elected him because they admired him for MAKING a fortune, not inheriting it. When the emperor is naked in this scenario, there is always the possibility that the downstairs will revolt and unite with each other against those upstairs. Or they might look at the other houses in the neighborhood—and perhaps decide that they have more in common with the downstairs in those houses than they do with their own upstairs housemates. All this could turn into a rejection of capitalism and a move downstairs toward some form of socialism or some other non-capitalist system.

If the downstairs withdraws its loyalty to the upstairs—and begins to identify with each other or with the downstairs in foreign lands, the house, in other words, could begin to crack. Solidarity across houses or national boundaries among the downstairs folks can threaten all capitalist houses—and the global capitalist system itself. The greatest danger for the upstairs is that the downstairs folks no longer feel identified with the house and begin to think of building their own new house and neighborhood.

Gramsci described the ruling creed (or in some case creeds since there can be more than one) as the cement of the capitalist house.[22] In the US, the leading creed is about the American Dream and American "exceptionalism." It is a set of ideas about merit, opportunity and freedom in the capitalist US house. The house must always manufacture the creed that unites upstairs and downstairs in their love of the house, the capitalist nation itself. For most of American history that creed has been the Meritocracy story—the story we flesh out shortly—that those living upstairs deserve to be there because they are smart, hardworking and blessed with all the "right stuff."

The Happy House

The legitimating creed of any house or society is fashioned by its elites—helped along by a sector of their PMC allies in the media, schools, churches and other social institutions. It justifies the house architecture and unites the downstairs working folk with the upstairs elites. The most essential work of the upstairs rulers is manufacturing the creed and embedding it in a larger legitimating strategy, the work that Edward Herman and the great social critic Noam Chomsky describe as "manufacturing consent."[23]

As shown in *Downton Abbey* and the original *Upstairs Downstairs* show, early 20th-century British capitalist houses did this legitimating work very effectively. Despite their hard work and humiliating and unchangeable subordinate positions, the servants never questioned the basic morality of the upstairs/downstairs architecture. The upstairs drew on ancient ideas of nobility and inherited worth that made it inconceivable to think about the servants becoming the lords. But in the US, while the creeds legitimating the house also draw on these pre-capitalist aristocratic notions of worth, the narrative took on new forms, integrating modern capitalist ideas and stories linked to individualism, social mobility and the American Dream. Horatio Alger joined Benjamin Franklin and the large cast of rags-to-riches characters in American lore, altering in some ways the European capitalist upstairs legitimating creed but never deviating from the basic idea that the upstairs naturally segregates the worthy from the unworthy downstairs. Ragged Dick, the hero in Horatio's famous novel, succeeds because of good character and hard work:

> Dick says, "I can't read much more'n a pig; and my writin' looks like hens' tracks. I don't want to grow up knowin' no more'n a four-year-old boy. If you'll teach me readin' and writin' evenin's, you shall sleep in my room every night."

(p. 135)

Dick studies with the same diligence and good humor he applies to his daily living. According to the narrator, Dick "had perseverance, and was not easily discouraged. He had made up his mind he must know more, and was not disposed to complain of the difficulty of the task" (p. 139). All this hard work pays off. When a grateful father wants to reward Dick, he learns about Dick's difficult history and recently acquired ability to write and calculate figures. The father hires Dick as a clerk, and he takes his first step toward financial success.

Alger's moral in this story is clear. Luck doesn't take the place of good character, initiative and an education. According to Gary Scharnhorst, Alger used the same basic outline in all his stories, drawing heavily on the models of Benjamin Franklin's Autobiography and Dickens's novels.[24]

The rags-to-riches stories—which are a big part of the Meritocracy creed—partly "work" in America because there are thousands of famous examples, both real and fictional.[25] Among them are some of our best known movie stars, CEOS and film characters, born in poverty and ending up wealthy beyond belief, including stars such as:[26]

Tom Cruise
Leonardo DiCaprio
LeBron James
Steve Jobs
Oprah
David Letterman
Sarah Jessica Parker
Colonel Sanders

And then there are the films, game shows, reality shows and TV series telling and celebrating the rags-to-riches story:[27]

Rocky
My Fair Lady
The Wolf of Wall Street
American Idol

Who Wants to be a Millionaire?
Queen for a Day
Slumdog Millionaire
Scarface

There are just enough real rags-to-riches stories that millions believe them and have faith that if they work hard they'll get the gold at the end of the rainbow. Since the rise of US industrial capitalism after the Civil War, the dominant US creed has always been the Meritocracy story. It makes the case that people end up in the upstairs or downstairs based on their merit, that is, the people who have the guts and brains to live the American Dream.[28] Everyone can be the super-rich inhabitants living upstairs—the talented individuals whose abilities and hard work have earned them a rightful place up top. Nobody wants to think they are the ones who will be stuck in the downstairs or in the basement because if you think that way you are stigmatizing yourself, believing that you lack the merit, ability or hard work that propels "the best people" upstairs, and who fuel the productivity that makes America great.

Thomas Piketty notes that in the 19th century and earlier eras, inequality was not justified by meritocracy but by the unquestioned rights of inheritance or divine nobility. The shift to meritocracy is a powerful new "democratic" justification or morality tale for the "winners" since it shifts blame on struggling majorities who don't have the "right stuff" to make it in a free society of opportunity for everyone:

> Modern meritocratic society, especially in the United States, is much harder on the losers, because it seeks to justify domination on the grounds of justice, virtue and merit, to say nothing of the insufficient productivity of those at the bottom . . . The world to come may well combine the worst of two past worlds: both very large inequality of inherited wealth and very high wage inequalities justified in terms of merit and productivity (claims with very little basis in fact, as noted).[29]

The Meritocracy story says that it is purely the individual—and his/her own efforts and character—that determines his or her ultimate position. Ayn Rand, again, expresses the individualistic ethos with the most unreserved panache:

> Look at history. Everything thing we have, every great achievement has come from the independent work of some independent mind. . . . It is an ancient conflict. It has another name: the individual against the collective.[30]

In contrast to the "great achievements" by the "independent minds" of the creatives, the unsuccessful majority are unworthy of the top. They are born as Rand's "parasites" and deserve their lower position on the first floor or basement. Any collective action to get upstairs— whether unionizing or resisting on the street—only threatens tyranny.[31]

The Meritocracy story puts a lot of emphasis on the stairways in the house. The tale is that the stairways are broad and accessible for all those who have the "right stuff" to move up. Many millions are moving up, demonstrating their talents, competitiveness and moral worth. A recent model is Dr. Ben Carson, born in the slums of Detroit but talented and motivated enough to become a famous neurosurgeon and later appointed by President Trump as Secretary of Housing and Urban Development. While such figures are lionized as proof of the Meritocracy story, bounding up the stairs, many millions downstairs are staying put where they were born, heads bowed, a sign that they have not lived up to the character that proves worthy of rising and living upstairs. And, as the great sociologist, Max Weber, has shown, our founding Puritans taught that we know whether God blessed us by our success—meaning that the upstairs is, in a sense, divinely selected.[32]

The PMC on the mezzanine helps reinforce the Meritocracy story, since many have gone to school and rise through what appears to be their own intellect and hard work. Interestingly, though, many working on the mezzanine serve or teach poor or uneducated clients in the downstairs or basement, and help foment a liberal or "Left" cultural counter-narrative to the Meritocracy story. Ironically, though, their working-class clients on the first floor often buy into the Meritocracy story anyway, rejecting the PMC and identifying instead with the capitalist upstairs. This is an integral part of the cultural wars playing out in the house, where a surprising alliance between the capitalist upstairs and the working-class downstairs joins against another alliance between the PMC mezzanine and the basement dwellers. Workers' uniting with capitalists reflects partly the cultural power that the PMC exercise, often unwittingly on its own behalf, engendering feelings of disrespect among masses of less-educated working people. This has ironies because the PMC, while invested in meritocracy, also offers counter-narratives to the upstairs/downstairs capitalist story that can help empower the down-stairs and basement.[33]

The capitalist house promotes in its meritocratic creed what Chuck Collins calls the myth of "*deservedness*," a way of describing America's individualistic ethos that we are entirely responsible for our own fate.[34] People rise or fall on the basis of their own individual merits, and end up where they are not because of their birth or any inherited advantage highlighted in *Downton Abbey* and the British *Upstairs Downstairs*. Only individualistic effort and inherent worth determines one's fate.

The story line of one's success touted by the fat and happy folks upstairs is that "I did it on my own." This view is widely shared throughout the house; as bestselling author, Malcolm Gladwell, writes "We cling to the idea that success is a simple function of individual merit and that the world in which we all grow up and the rules we choose to write as a society don't matter at all."[35] Any fair person would embrace this house because it justly rewards people for their sacred personal abilities, competitiveness and character.

In a wonderful book, Collins notes that he was "born on third base" into the wealthy Oscar Mayer family of meatpackers, giving him advantages that made him question the Meritocracy story and the individualistic deservedness myth.[36] His own story made him realize that some people are born with tailwinds—such as the great schools, money and social contacts he got from mom and dad—driving his 1% compatriots forward to ever more wealth (though Collins actually gave up his fortune as a young man) while others face strong headwinds blowing them back. Collins has a great story about his "aha!" moment connecting inequality to the idea of tail- and headwinds. He was riding his bike South on a Cape Cod Rail Trail and pedaled the first 10 miles faster than he thought he could. He says "I feel great. . . . I'm in better shape than I thought." But then he turns around to return and everything changes after pedaling back a couple of miles:

> I feel depleted. I stop for a drink of water. . . . I realize that the subtle wind has probably been constant but I hadn't noticed it before. On the first part of my ride, the wind was at my back and I was oblivious. Now that it's in my face I can't ignore it. After another 2 miles riding into the wind, I'm exhausted . . .

> Lying in the grass, waiting for a ride, I laugh at myself, and at the apt metaphor for privilege. Privilege is like a wind at my back, propelling me forward. Of course, I'm pedaling so I can claim some credit for my forward motion. But the wind makes an enormous difference. And here I thought it was all me.[37]

Collins says his peak performance with the tailwind made him feel "I did it myself," the classic American idea of success. Only when he realized the role of tail- and headwinds on the bike, did he see in a new way the flaws of the deservedness and meritocratic myth. The meritocracy story can grow only out of illusions of equal opportunity and pure personal responsibility, and in the Happy House, millions on both the upstairs and downstairs never think about the headwinds and the tailwinds.

The deservedness creed intersects with the ancient pre-capitalist myths of nobility and legitimacy and the early British capitalist creed, both on display in *Upstairs Downstairs* and *Downton Abbey*. Both ultimately draw on stories of the worthy and unworthy, which as we show in Chapter 2, have roots in the aristocratic order of European feudalism governed by lords. The meritocracy story is intertwined with this ancient story, and threatens today less a return to feudalism than to authoritarian capitalism and new forms of neo-fascism.

The Meritocracy story, while more widely questioned today after the Occupy Wall Street movement and the growth of extreme inequality, remains persuasive to millions of Americans—and it does more than justify where each individual is living in the house. It shows that the upstairs/downstairs architecture is essential for the moral character of the house itself. If everyone lived under the same general conditions on the same floor, it would not allow the "creatives" with more talent or moral character to be rewarded for their virtues. It would undermine freedom itself, that is, the freedom to fulfill and be rewarded for one's potential, thus sabotaging the prosperity of the capitalist house as well as eroding personal happiness, liberty and morality.[38]

Meritocracy turns the upstairs/downstairs architecture—and thus the inequality built into the capitalist house—into a supreme moral virtue. Though it has to ward off cultural challenges from parts of the PMC and the basement, such legitimating dominant morality has historically done its job well. *It breeds consent to the house precisely because of its meritocratic inequality.* In a capitalist nation like the US, the deservedness narrative sustains the house and breeds love for both the nation and the capitalist system. And it is this love that unifies the upstairs and downstairs.

Since this is happening in many other capitalist houses in the neighborhood, it is legitimating both the nation and the global order. The inhabitants in each house—both upstairs and downstairs—are pledging allegiance to their own nation; thus we have been describing essentially the underpinnings of capitalist nationalism. But since the upstairs classes are working together to sustain the global neighborhood, we are also discussing the legitimation of capitalist globalism.

This makes clear that modern capitalism must be understood as *national globalism*. It simultaneously creates a capitalism that is both nationalist and globalist.

The Real House

The happy house discussed previously is an idealized picture. While elites have been presenting it as a truthful portrait for many decades, it is misleading, especially for today's design. In the last few decades, since the rise of the Reagan revolution, the real house is such a far cry from the reality that even elites have taken note and are working to change the house creed and the legitimating ideology before the house crashes down around them.

The truth is that the house architecture is changing profoundly in a way that creates new dangers for the house stability and legitimacy. The house, of course, is still very much an upstairs-downstairs structure. All the floors and rooms are still there. At first glance, the basic design looks similar to the "happy" model.

But a closer look reveals some big changes. The distance between the upstairs and downstairs is widening. The upstairs is more affluent, even aristocratic, in its décor; it is a high-tech version of the aristocratic *Downton Abbey* upstairs. About 160,000 US households occupying the penthouses of the upstairs—the top .1% of the top 1%—are seeing their wealth growing far faster than the downstairs 90%, in fact faster than any other part of the population.[39] Thomas Piketty shows that if current rate of wealth concentration in the top 1% continues, they will own 50% of all US wealth by 2030, compared to 35% in 2011—while the bottom 50% owned only 2% of national wealth and its miniscule wealth continues to shrink.[40]

The PMC on the Mezzanine is also doing just fine. As Atlantic journalist, Matthew Stewart, a self-identified PMC success, writes about his class today:

> By any sociological or financial measure, it's good to be us. It's even better to be our kids. In our health, family life, friendship

networks, and level of education, not to mention money, we are crushing the competition below . . . (our) meritocratic class has mastered the old trick of consolidating wealth and passing privilege along at the expense of other people's children.[41]

The PMC, like the CEOS, has ever stronger tailwinds propelling them forward, by virtue of the money and elite schooling provided courtesy of mom and dad.

The downstairs is moving in the opposite direction, less well off than portrayed in the happy house, and drifting closer to the drab servant quarters of *Downton Abbey*. It is full of servile residents who seem to be working harder but have little chance of climbing the stairs to the top and a much bigger chance of falling into the basement. The headwinds faced by the downstairs are becoming hurricane force, as if churned up by climate change storms.

Look only at the staircases. They are narrower than they seem in the happy house picture—and they are shrinking. There is less space on the staircase for people to move up from the downstairs to the upstairs. And the number of people moving up is shrinking, along with the size of the staircases.

Economists can now document this narrowing staircase. The future position of an American child is increasingly determined by the income or position of their parents, a statistical finding that is so important that it is worth citing in detail, as summarized in 2018 by journalist Matthew Stewart:

> Imagine yourself on the socioeconomic ladder with one end of a rubber band around your ankle and the other around your parents' rung. The strength of the rubber determines how hard it is for you to escape the rung on which you were born. If your parents are high on the ladder, the band will pull you up should you fall; if they are low, it will drag you down when you start to rise. Economists represent this concept with a number they call "intergenerational earnings elasticity," or IGE, which measures how much of a

child's deviation from average income can be accounted for by the parents' income. An IGE of zero means that there's no relationship at all between parents' income and that of their offspring. An IGE of one says that the destiny of a child is to end up right where she came into the world.

According to Miles Corak, an economics professor at the City University of New York, half a century ago IGE in America was less than 0.3. Today, it is about 0.5. In America, the game is half over once you've selected your parents. IGE is now higher here than in almost every other developed economy. On this measure of economic mobility, the United States is more like Chile or Argentina than Japan or Germany.[42]

On the other hand, the chute from the downstairs to the basement has gotten wider. More people downstairs are falling down the chute, at the very time that fewer people in the upstairs are falling downstairs. These downward slides—or fear of losing everything—are producing the first generation of American men who are living less long than their fathers. And even middle-class students worry that student debt will always keep them in the downstairs no matter how hard they work.

Fear of plunging into the basement if they get sick or lose their job—or simply see their wages drop—increasingly terrifies millions of Americans on the first floor. This anxiety of the "precariat" on the first floor is an explosive part of American politics, a working-class fear historically thought to benefit liberals or the Left but—partly because of the magical legitimating stories spun by the upstairs—also very much the fuel of conservative and Far Right movements, including Trumpism and other white nationalist or neo-fascist movements that are transforming both the US and Europe.

The vast and growing differences in the conditions upstairs and downstairs—as well as the shrinking of the staircases—are a profound change in the house design. The happy house rests on the view that the upstairs and downstairs are not so different as to threaten their ability to live in the same house and world. And wide stair-cases demonstrate that all the house people who have the right stuff to climb up can do so. But as the staircase structure narrows sig-nificantly, this undercuts the meritocratic creed of the house and thus threatens the house's very foundation, including the idea of the American Dream itself.

The staircases have never been as wide as portrayed in the Happy House picture and the Meritocracy story. But their current shrinkage—and the more glaring difference now in the aristocratic conditions of the upstairs relevant to the declining conditions downstairs—reflects structural changes put in place since the Reagan revolution. Ironically, they intensify the upstairs-downstairs division that defines the house's basic design or architecture. But taken to an extreme, the upstairs/downstairs division undermines the Happy House's solidarity and its meritocracy creed, requiring a new creed—or more broadly a new strategy to legitimate and unite the house—to keep it from cracking apart.

These growing upstairs/downstairs divisions help fuel the progressive counter-narratives promoted by sectors of the PMC and their clients in the basement. It is so far from the downstairs to the upstairs—and the stairs are so much narrower—that meritocracy, mobility and the American Dream seem, well, just a dream. The PMC and Left critique of meritocracy offered by critics such as Collins gains more traction as the distance between the upstairs and downstairs becomes virtually insurmountable.

The design changes in our metaphorical house reflect the extreme growth of inequality in the real world. Since the election of President Reagan in 1980, a set of economic, political, technological and cultural changes have fueled a major shift of fortune all across the capitalist world to the wealthiest class and a stagnation of the income and wealth going to most other people.

Because the ratio of CEO to average worker pay is a strong indica-tor of the distance between upstairs and downstairs, look at the CEO and average worker pay in some major US companies, documented at payscale.com[43]

Company Name	CEO	Median Worker Annual Pay (Cash)	CEO Annual Pay (Cash)	Pay Ratio (Cash)	Total CEO Compensation	% of CEO Comp That Is Cash
CVS Health Corp	Larry J. Merlo	$27,900	$12,105,481	434:1	$22,855,374	53%
CBS Corp	Leslie Moonves	$59,900	$23,652,883	395:1	$56,352,801	42%
Walt Disney CO/	Robert A. Iger	$71,400	$26,208,003	367:1	$43,490,567	60%
TJX Companies Inc /DE/	Carol Meyrowitz	$22,400	$7,330,584	327:1	$17,962,232	41%
Twenty-First Century Fox, Inc.	K. Rupert Murdoch	$54,800	$17,047,636	311:1	$22,192,923	77%
Comcast Corp	Brian L. Roberts	$55,800	$16,819,942	301:1	$27,520,744	61%
L Brands, Inc.	Leslie H. Wexner	$33,900	$9,665,925	285:1	$26,669,306	36%
Honeywell International Inc	David M. Cote	$81,600	$22,767,851	279:1	$33,105,851	69%
PepsiCo Inc	Indra K. Nooyi	$61,500	$15,937,828	259:1	$22,189,307	72%
Wynn Resorts Ltd	Stephen A. Wynn	$50,100	$11,930,391	238:1	$20,680,391	58%
Goodyear Tire & Rubber Co /OH/	Richard J. Kramer	$54,700	$12,779,784	234:1	$17,772,128	72%
Allergan Plc	Brenton L. Saunders	$92,900	$21,565,325	232:1	$21,565,325	100%
Viacom Inc.	Philippe P. Dauman	$79,400	$18,263,525	230:1	$54,140,509	34%
Cablevision Systems Corp /NY	James L. Dolan	$62,000	$13,649,028	220:1	$24,539,725	56%
Liberty Media & Liberty Interactive	Gregory B. Maffei	$51,100	$10,947,607	214:1	$26,868,931	41%
Wal Mart Stores Inc.	C. Douglas McMillon	$24,600	$5,133,256	209:1	$19,404,042	26%

In 2018, a congressionally mandated vast study by the Security and Exchange Commission, called "Rewarding or Hoarding," based on 225 large corporations with annual revenues of $6.3 trillion and with 14 million workers, showed an astonishing CEO/worker pay ratio of 339 to 1. The highest gap was nearly 5,000 to 1.[44]

In 219 of the companies, the average worker would have to work 45 years to make what their top boss makes in one year. In the fast food and retail sector, the average ratio was 977 to 1. The study, released publicly by Minnesota Congressperson Keith Ellison, showed that these astounding ratios existed even in companies with poor economic performance, not reflecting extraordinary talent on the part of the executives; moreover, the ratios understate the real gap because it did not include the lower wages of employees hired by the companies abroad.[45]

The *Wall Street Journal* notes that the current CEO/worker pay ratio has soared tenfold over the last 40 years, from 30 to 1 to the current 300+ to 1.[46] According to Piketty, this is not hard to understand because CEO salaries do not get set by a free market or reflect productivity but

> are set by the executive themselves. . . . It may be excessive to accuse senior executives of having their hands in the till, but the metaphor is probably more apt than Adam Smith's metaphor of the "invisible hand."[47]

The shift toward nearly unbearable inequality over recent decades, ironically, helped elect Donald Trump, who would make things worse. Many white working-class voters understood they needed something entirely new—perhaps even the blowhard billionaire Trump—to stem the economic and cultural abandonment and betrayal they were feeling as jobs became more insecure, wages stagnated and the distance between upstairs and downstairs became impossible to bridge. Trump was hardly their savior but he did touch a raw nerve, tapping not only into the downstairs economic anxiety but into the cultural anger and populist resentment growing among white "Reagan Democrats" and Trumpist workers who were falling into the basement while neither the Republican nor Democratic Establishment was doing anything to help them.

After the 1960s, corporate America teamed up with culturally conservative white working people and rural folk in an exceptionally successful alliance that has defied analysis and common sense. The corporate New Right in the 1970s brilliantly orchestrated a movement to end the New Deal by mobilizing its very beneficiaries—the downstairs working class and rural folks—into a new alliance with the CEO class upstairs. Why sectors of the downstairs turned against their own economic interests has become one of the great questions of our era—with answers rooted not only in the emotional resonance of ancient and resurfacing legitimating stories by the Right but also stories and strategies by the Left and the PMC that alienated, neglected or disrespected large sectors of the downstairs.

After Reagan's election in 1980, the upstairs created a regime change fueling today's inequality tsunami—while they re-crafted legitimating stories with deep and resonant roots in the downstairs. The economic strategy is now depressingly familiar and institutionally enshrined: accelerate globalization and outsource jobs to drastically cheapen labor costs, exploit technology and the robotics revolution to eliminate jobs and create downstairs workers desperate enough to take massive pay cuts, demolish unions to reduce downstairs bargaining power, massively reduce taxes on the rich to increase upstairs income and wealth, lock in austerity policies that destroy social welfare and turn upward mobility into a fantasy for most in the basement or first floor, all while crafting house creeds and legitimating stories with powerful emotional resonance downstairs.[48]

Today's inequality is, indeed, extreme, and it represents a major shift in direction from the New Deal. But it represents the return of deep inequality that has long defined almost all capitalist societies. Piketty's data show that deep and growing inequality has predominated in all capitalist nations almost all the time (with the Western mid-20th-century era the main exception). Piketty explained this by showing that since 1700, the return to capital owned by the upstairs averaged about 5% relative to a return to labor or wage growth averaging about 1–2%, with deep permanent inequality also reflecting the ability of the upstairs to manipulate the market and set their own salaries.[49] This leads Piketty to the conclusion that the upstairs are a new kind of capitalist aristocracy, creating conditions of permanent inequality and wealth that make a mockery of the American Dream and the creed of meritocracy.

Piketty summarizes:

> The conditions are ideal for an "inheritance society" to prosper—where by "inheritance society" I mean a society characterized by both a very high concentration of wealth and a significant persistence of large fortunes from generation to generation.[50]

Piketty shows that inherited wealth in the US is already at least 50% of total US capital or wealth, with some arguing more like 70% to 80%.[51] Because wealth has been highly concentrated in capitalism—with the majority of Americans having little or no wealth—we are destined, Piketty argues, to move in the 21st century toward a *capitalist aristocracy*, a term that everyone needs to absorb because it runs against the widespread belief that we live in a democracy very different than medieval aristocratic societies. Piketty puts the argument in dry but stark terms:

> People with inherited wealth need save only a portion of their income from capital to see that capital grow more quickly than the economy as a whole. Under such conditions, it is almost inevitable that inherited wealth will dominate wealth amassed from a lifetime's labor by a wide margin, and the concentration of capital exceed extremely high levels—levels potentially incompatible with the meritocratic values and principles of social justice incompatible with democratic society.[52]

This helps explain why *Downton Abbey* and *Upstairs Downstairs* strike a nerve in 21st-century post-modern high-tech capitalism. Despite all the obvious changes in the last several centuries ushered in by highly dynamic and technologically innovative capitalist societies, humans over many centuries have inhabited upstairs/downstairs societies ruled by types of nobility, who steer accumulating great wealth to themselves. The capitalist elites today reincarnate a 21st-century model of aristocracy, a view based on the long history of the capitalist house that Piketty, no Marxist himself, has documented to the satisfaction of most economists. Those who deny Piketty's findings are something like climate change deniers, closing their eyes to well-established realities.

Two important conclusions stand out. One is that legitimacy is a permanent problem in capitalism, even in the most affluent capitalist houses such as the US today, since an extreme and deepening divide between upstairs and downstairs is making the meritocratic legitimation story harder and harder to believe. Capitalist aristocrats who increasingly pass their wealth and real estate in the upstairs to their heirs are building a new society based to a large degree on heredity rather than merit or hard work (though many of these elites do, indeed, work hard as well). Capitalism is resurrecting a potentially mortal contradiction between its reality and mythology.

Second, it suggests that the upstairs will turn back to much older legitimation stories to keep the house united, since extreme inequality goes back to the beginning of capitalism (or even before). Many legitimating stories—and most notably the Security story, a dark and divisive narrative revolving around fear and tribalism that is the subject of much of this book—were created centuries ago and have long helped the divided house, with aristocracies and inherited wealth, survive and thrive. Their success makes these ancient stories attractive to the upstairs again, and they have long played a role in legitimating capitalist societies, including the US. They have always carried great danger for democratic societies. And they are now resurfacing with a vengeance, casting dark and violent shadows. They hint at new forms of authoritarian and aristocratic societies, whether "strongman" capitalist regimes or neo-fascist societies we now see rising in parts of Europe and possibly in the US itself.

2

SELLING SECURITY FOR HONOR AND PROFIT

THE STORY LINKING ANCIENT WITH CAPITALIST ARISTOCRACIES

God save our gracious Queen
Long live our noble Queen!
God save the Queen!
Send her victorious,
Happy and glorious,
Long to reign over us,
God save the Queen.
O Lord our God arise,
Scatter her enemies
And make them fall;
Confound their politics,
Frustrate their knavish tricks,
On Thee our hopes we fix,
God save us all![1]

—British National Anthem

God gave me my money. I believe the power to make money is a gift from God to be developed and used to the best of our ability for the good of mankind.

—John D. Rockefeller

> We are royalty.
> —Cal Hockley (Billy Zane) millionaire businessman in the
> film, *Titanic*

Do people crave leaders who may actually oppress them? One of the most debated questions in the US is why did so many workers vote for a billionaire, Donald Trump, who opposed unions, fought a minimum wage, cut spending on education, Medicare and job training, and in every way seemed to oppose workers' own self-interests? This same question can be asked more broadly about the majority of white people downstairs, people like "Joe the Plumber" who became famous in the 2008 presidential race when he stood up in Ohio rallies and denounced Obama for saying "when you spread the wealth around, it's good for everyone." Joe, a conservative guy who has bounced around a lot of jobs but never actually became a plumber, denounced this as socialist treason, and the Republicans turned "the Plumber" into a hero. Millions of working people like Joe have been voting for anti-worker Republicans for 40 years, starting with Ronald Reagan.

Donald Trump has bragged he "could shoot somebody on Fifth Avenue" in New York and not lose the support of his base (of Joe the Plumber, other Rust Belt angry white working people as well as many of the upstairs rich corporate elites who delightedly signaled their love of Joe). At this writing, more than a year and a half after his election, it seems Trump was right.

Joe the Plumber, whose real name is Samuel Joseph Wurzelbacher, cashed in on media interest in Rust Belt folk like him, has written a book and created a blog with 100,000 followers. He has been happy to tell the media why he, and people like him, are drawn to Trump:

> He's a winner. He's made billions. He's dated beautiful women. His wife is a model. That's not to sniff at. And a lot of people believe he can bring that kind of success to the White House.[2]

And with a gun by his side, Joe tells a journalist, hinting at the Security story we will tell in this chapter. He says:

> the more people who have guns the safer they will be.[3]

And Joe wants to put those guns to use on the border to increase national safety, yelling at one GOP rally:

> put troops on the border going to Mexico and start shooting I bet that solves our immigration problem real quick.[4]

Karl Marx thought the workers would rise up against the Trumps of the world: "workers of the world unite" are the words emblazoned on Marx's tombstone. And they still might rise up. Many workers, including white workers, hate Trump. Trump's base—full of hedge fund managers, CEOs and many small business owners as well as evangelicals—has a median income of about $72,000, much higher than the average worker. Many college-educated whites are part of Trump's base, contrary to popular mythology. In June, 2018, the *New York Times* noted that:

> According to a Pew Research survey this month, approximately 31 percent of Trump approvers are white men without a college degree, and 66 percent are either college graduates, women or nonwhite. . . . According to Gallup, Mr. Trump's popularity with college-educated voters has remained about equal to his popularity with Americans overall this year.[5]

Nonetheless, many blue-collar white workers in the Rust Belt helped push Trump over the line into the White House.

Marx was a brilliant analyst of the capitalist system, but his crystal ball got blurry when he tried to see how ordinary people would react to the extreme inequality he predicted. The idea of a *capitalist-worker alliance*, that began to emerge most recently in the Reagan era and continues to grow in the Age of Trump, drives the neo-Marxist Left crazy, and suggests we need to understand a lot more about how Americans think and feel if we are ever to get to a more socially just society.

Part of the problem is that how Americans think is shaped by propaganda which has become both cruder and more sophisticated in recent decades. The capitalist upstairs is ratcheting up a new/old ruling story to bolster a weakened meritocracy story and win over a downstairs looking at its American Dream disappear.

We call it the Security story. It's a very old story that is perhaps the most common in history, especially in societies built on deep inequality. The Security story appeared in antiquity and in the Middle Ages, justifying the rule of ancient emperors, kings and queens and medieval nobility. It has also been a powerful, emotionally resonating story through most eras of capitalism. But while one of the earliest and enduring ruling narratives, it's also a new story because it's been adapted to the still very unequal but unique economy and morality of 21st-century global capitalism.

The long history of the Security story testifies to its intense appeal as an emotional narrative, responding to strong irrational currents in human consciousness and deep visceral feelings involving fear, survival and respect. First, it legitimates the upstairs by "selling" safety to the downstairs; think just of Joe the Plumber talking about how people like him feel safe only with as many guns as possible and shooting at enemies who are asylum seekers crossing at the border. The Security story talks about numerous enemies that threaten the downstairs and the very survival of individuals and the house itself. It justifies the authority of the upstairs as the only force that can guarantee security for all. It identifies the main external and internal enemies that threaten the downstairs and shows how the upstairs protects those below them. It is a new version of a "protection racket" that ruling elites have used throughout history.

In the famous novel, *1984*, George Orwell made perhaps the greatest description of a society run and justified by a Security story. The dictator, loved by all as Big Brother, ruled Oceania, an empire at war with two other empires, Eurasia and Eastasia. Oceania state propaganda about the two evil empires flooded the population on omnipresent "telescreens." Fearing and fighting these enemies was everything. As Orwell put it, "to die hating them, that was freedom."[6]

Hate and fear of the enemy bonded everyone together with Big Brother, who was the only one who could protect them from the ever-present frightening enemy. The regime ginned up fear and hatred by daily state rituals called the "two minutes hate." His description has become iconic:

The Hate had started. As usual, the face of Emmanuel Goldstein, the Enemy of the People, had flashed on to the screen.

The Party's modus operandi in maintaining power is to shift blame to a designated scapegoat, toward which all of its constituents' hatred and violence may be directed. Their favorite scapegoat is up today—Emmanuel Goldstein.

In its second minute the Hate rose to a frenzy. People were leaping up and down in their places and shouting at the tops of their voices in an effort to drown the maddening bleating voice that came from the screen. The little sandy-haired woman had turned bright pink, and her mouth was opening and shutting like that of a landed fish. Even O'Brien's heavy face was flushed. He was sitting very straight in his chair, his powerful chest swelling and quivering as though he were standing up to the assault of a wave. The dark-haired girl behind Winston had begun crying out "Swine! Swine! Swine!" and suddenly she picked up a heavy Newspeak dictionary and flung it at the screen.

The Party's go-to tactic for maintaining power is to shift blame to a designated scapegoat, toward which all of its constituents' hatred and violence may be directed. Here we have the citizens letting it all out during the daily Two Minutes Hate—which is of course organized and overseen by the Party.[7]

The Security story—in capitalist and in Big Brother authoritarian regimes—goes beyond identifying enemies to often manufacturing them. Some threats to the house and individuals are real. But inventing or inflating enemies is integral to the American and most other Security stories, which since the Soviet Revolution involved vastly exaggerating the Communist threat and protecting the public from "the evil Empire."

Indeed, Noam Chomsky has written about the Cold War that if the Soviet Union had not existed, the US would have had to invent it. Chomsky doesn't mean that the US secretly loved the Soviets. But US elites found them incredibly useful as an enemy to mobilize and unite the downstairs with the upstairs. Chomsky writes that there has long been intense propaganda about necessary enemies. He describes the propaganda as well funded and ever more sophisticated, drawn from marketing and public relations experts such as Joseph Bernays, to "manufacture consent," or scare the public into submission, taking the forms of hate and fear campaigns something like those described by Orwell. They have been:

> quite self-conscious campaigns by business . . . to curb dissent. The ideology of anti-Communism has served this purpose since World War I . . .

> In earlier years, Woodrow Wilson's Red Scare demolished unions and other dissident elements. A prominent feature was the suppression of independent politics and free speech.[8]

In the Cold War, US leaders ratcheted up to an incredibly high level "a frightening portrayal of the Communist threat, in order to overcome [US public] dissent."[9] Protection from the Communist threat, later to be supplanted by protection from Islamic terrorists, was the hot molten core of the rising American Security story as the Meritocracy story weakened in credibility. It was a fear story about enemies that seemed one of the only ways to distract the downstairs from their economic anxieties.

The relation between the US elites and the Soviet elites, as described by Chomsky and the Security story, was what Oprah calls "co-dependent:" the two Superpowers hated each other but saw the enemy as essential to their own survival. Manufacturing or exaggerating threats is a key way to bolster the Security story, part of the reason it can be seen as part of a "protection racket," and it has always been a major part of the legitimating strategy of the capitalist upstairs, especially in the US.

The Security story works because it not only comforts in the face of fear, real or imagined, but also offers a sense of worth, respect and inclusion in the tribe or nation to all who feel worthless and disrespected. The story helps reconstruct the house as a protective community for all— downstairs and upstairs—who truly belong. It also promises to purge those who are not really part of the tribe or nation—the internal enemy or imposter residents secretly tied to frightening external enemies. The

Security story is thus also an emotionally riveting story of the tribe and nation—one that builds safety and respect through a process of exclusion and purification, distinguishing the true members of the tribe or house from "those people" who don't belong. It is intimately linked to an emotional and tribal nationalism that makes capitalism the system we call national globalism.

The Security story has two special dimensions that need emphasis from the beginning. First, it is a story about the overwhelming importance of strong (if not strongman) upstairs authority. Such authority requires obedience or deference but in exchange it delivers security from terrible enemies and fears, real or imagined. The upstairs insists that its ruling authority be accepted, but its Security story claims that the downstairs is getting more than its fair share of the bargain.

The claim of such legitimate authority may seem contradictory to American democratic norms, and there are tensions between security and democracy, which became widely discussed in the US after 9/11. Islamic fundamentalist attacks made the Security story much more credible, and led millions of Americans to say that elites upstairs needed more authority and deference to guarantee national security (think the Patriot Act and FISA courts authorizing spying on Americans). But this is only part of a broader struggle in capitalism to legitimate a house that is formally democratic but ruled by an autocratic upstairs concentrating power in itself in the name of security.

The Ancient History of the Security Story

The upstairs Security story rests on the understanding that strong authority is like Elmer's glue for unequal and unjust societies. American capitalism has rejected official kings and queens, but it never abandoned the pre-capitalist understanding that the more insecure people feel, the more they may rely on upstairs authority to feel safe. The famed social critic and student of the authoritarian personality, Erich Fromm, argued that there might be an "instinctive" basis for such willing submission to the authority upstairs:

> Is there not also, perhaps, besides an innate desire for freedom, an instinctive wish for submission? If there is not, how can we

account for the attraction which submission to a leader has for so many to-day? . . . Is there a hidden satisfaction in submitting, and what is its essence?[10]

Conservative philosophers have argued that survival *requires* submission to absolutist authority. Reacting to the beheading of British 17th-century monarch, Charles I, Thomas Hobbes argued the first duty of the sovereign is to protect his subjects by being so brutal that nobody dares challenge him. Only if the king is strong enough to kill you can he be strong enough to protect you and other anxious people downstairs. By being unable to prevent his own beheading, Charles I showed he was weak and therefore unfit.

The Security story rests on ancient and enduring religious and political ideas expressing the necessity and goodness of hierarchy. Philosopher Karl Mannheim argues that submission to superior people has been accepted through most of human history:

> In pre-democratic society, all social authority is inextricably linked to the idea of the ontological superiority of the wielder of authority. No person, family or institution can exert authority without being regarded as made of "higher" stuff than the ordinary run of humanity.[11]

Historically, such authority has been seen as divinely ordained. In the New Testament, Romans Chapter 13 starts like this:

> Let every person be subject to the governing authorities. For there is no authority except from God, and those that exist have been instituted by God. Therefore he who resists the authorities resists what God has appointed, and those who resist will incur judgment. For rulers are not a terror to good conduct, but to bad.[12]

Aristotle also discussed the notion of a great and natural hierarchy that Thomas Aquinas, the medieval theologian, would describe as "The Great Chain of Being." Mannheim wrote of the Chain that it is a hierarchy designed by God himself, placing everything in a "finite" universe in a particular place in an ascending chain. It states that the more spirit something has, the higher it is placed on the chain. The Chain, as a metaphor, had a long and highly influential tenure.

The chain was developed based on Aristotle's *scala natura* (Natural Ladder) theory, and kept the balance of the world in check. Any disturbance would carry throughout the entire chain and affect all levels. There was no mobility in the ranks of the Chain, and no additions to the life forms represented either.[13]

The Great Chain of Being described a hierarchy with God, Angels, Kings/Queens and Archbishops at the top, with Priests, Squires, Pages, Messengers, Shopkeepers and Farmers in the Middle, and Household Servants, Tenant Farmers, Thieves, Gypsies, Birds, Worms and Rocks at the bottom.[14] The Security story plays off the Great Chain of Being, in which upstairs authority rules. The secret to winning downstairs loyalty is promising protection to those unable to protect themselves. The Great Chain of Being is the archetype of all Right-wing legitimating narratives, appealing at a gut level to the needs of the downstairs workers for safety and respect.

A Security story that surrenders too much power to authority can undermine capitalist rhetorical ideals of individual empowerment and democracy, taken seriously by the majority of the population. In 21st-century America, many millions hate the authoritarian bullying of President Trump, who acts like a King unchecked by anybody. But leading groups on the upstairs are more than prepared to expand authority at the expense of freedom when its profits and very survival are at stake. Moreover, these elites recognize that many in the downstairs feel more secure with a "strong man" who would enshrine new respect for ruling power in a society that seemed to be declining and facing chaos.

While cautious not to explicitly throw out all reason and democracy, the rising Security story makes the upstairs authority—the 21st-century capitalist Aristocracy—the indispensable rock of Gibraltar, protecting all of us. As the Meritocracy story weakens and the Security story becomes the stronger legitimating narrative, the entire capitalist house becomes vulnerable to a shift toward ancient, more authoritarian systems. The Security story helps guide capitalism toward a new/old model: perhaps a modern aristocratic feudalism or even fascism, a prospect that increasingly terrifies many in both the US and Europe.

Manufacturers, CEOs and Wall Street bankers are conflicted because capitalism depends on rationality as the basis of science and technology that propels economic innovation and growth, as well as underlies democracy. Reason and respect for science are essential to capitalist development, leading to long historical struggles between science and religion—or between rationality and irrationality—in capitalist societies. Some capitalist upstairs elites, particularly in Silicon Valley and other high-tech industries, reject the more extreme and irrational versions of the Security story pedaled by President Trump because they recognize the special importance of science and reason to their own form of capitalism.

Religion—which Marx famously called "the opium of the masses"— is the archetype of "irrationality," a way of thinking that regards faith rather than reason as the basis for all aspects of social life and authority. It is no surprise that the capitalist upstairs has turned to Evangelical Christians to champion its Security story. As we explore shortly, societies based on religion reject rationality and empirical evidence as the basis for truth and objective fact. Before capitalism, medieval feudalism prized religion over science and grounded life in faith and emotion that were their own justification. If I have faith—or "feel it," then it is true, a mantra of feudal religious and irrational culture.

In contrast, capitalism celebrates science, belief in empirical evidence and technological rationality; these are the basis of prosperity and truth. But it has also always had its own form of irrationality, involving greed and almost religious faith in the market. In its turn to the Security story, the capitalist house is turning ever more toward irrationality and emotion. The rising Security story rests largely on an appeal to emotions, especially fear and the need for respect. It resonates with the downstairs because it promises an antidote to paralyzing fear from external and internal enemies in the house. And it also delivers respect—by protecting and purifying the tribal house—not only by delivering national security from terrifying foreign enemies but purging imposters and internal enemies who have been disrespecting the downstairs. The Security story always involves "purification"—a story of excluding the imposters contaminating the greatness of the tribe.

These internal enemies—targeted for purging and exclusion by the US Security story—are racial outsiders of the American tribe. They are people of color and immigrants flooding over the border, and also the liberal Democrats and the highly educated PMC on the mezzanine who ally with these outsiders and dismiss many white workers downstairs as uneducated bigots or know-nothings.

Republicans use the Security story to champion the white workers as the true tribe. They point to President Obama's famous disparaging comment in 2008 about them:

> They get bitter, they cling to guns or religion or antipathy to people who aren't like them or anti-immigrant sentiment or anti-trade sentiment as a way to explain their frustrations.[15]

Hillary Clinton labeled them *"deplorables."*[16] Many analysts believe these words turned the 2016 election to Trump, a sign of how liberal Democratic arrogance and "disrespect" cuts deep into working-class sensibilities and how the Security story restores feelings of dignity to them. This harkens back to the comedian Rodney Dangerfield's famous self-lament:

> Can't get no respect!

The working class and their upstairs bosses knew what Dangerfield was talking about. The upstairs Security story props up the downstairs psychological as well as physical security. Trump understood that "America First" signaled to the downstairs Americans that they were the greatest!

The Right has historically understood—better than the Left—the irrationality and emotions that govern politics, spinning legitimating stories that emotionally resonate deeply to the fear and need for respect in large parts of the capitalist downstairs. European fascism relied on it at its core. So did the New Right of the early 1970s. When it linked the capitalist aristocracy upstairs to the base of Evangelical Christians and "forgotten" white workers downstairs, it forged a union based less on rational self-interest than on irrational and mystical powers of tribe, nation and godly authority.

Capitalism has strong incentives—particularly high-tech capitalism—to reinforce its own calculated rationality and limit the Security story's form of irrational tribalism and opposition to the dry rationality of science. There is thus a great paradox in the new legitimating strategy of capitalism, which is trading off some of its core values to ensure unity and legitimacy among the great unwashed and irrational downstairs. But the Security story is now rising forcefully enough that it threatens the very survival of both capitalism and democracy, with a greater reliance on feudal residues in capitalism and, as just seen, potential shifts to authoritarian rule.

Feudalism's Security Story: Uniting Lords and Serfs

Before turning to the Security story in capitalism, it is worth moving forward from antiquity and looking briefly at feudalism and its Security story in the Middle Ages. This was the era from the 9th century to the 15th century—where aristocrats ruled and merchants were seen as unwashed heretics. The feudal Security story is worth telling because it offers insight into the narrative itself and why it is so emotionally resonant to the downstairs even today. Furthermore, capitalism itself grew out of feudalism, largely as a rebellion against it but perpetuating covertly many feudal residues.

Feudalism evolved into capitalism, as medieval baronies eventually were consolidated into the first large modern nation states subject to kings and queens. Beginning in early 16th-century England when Henry VIII confiscated church property and forced nobles to swear loyalty to the crown or lose their heads, a transitional era of "*absolutism*" developed. It melded feudal and capitalist attributes, since it saw the emergence of the modern capitalist bourgeoisie, as merchants of commerce began taking over resources from feudal landholders, as well as the growth of all-powerful state monarchies. The absolutist era—which some historians call "late feudalism" and lasted from the 16th to the 18th century—had a Security story derived from and similar to the medieval feudal story—and then passed on in new form to us today. Absolutism—a tyranny George Orwell understood in his bones—reveals how ancient feudal threads of fear and authoritarianism grew deep into our own modern democratic societies.

While feudalism and capitalism are profoundly different systems, they are both upstairs/downstairs societies based on extreme inequality. Power and wealth are overwhelmingly concentrated in the upstairs, though in capitalism the rhetoric is democratic and the downstairs can aspire to some social and political influence. Nonetheless, as economist Thomas Piketty has shown, as discussed in Chapter 1, the capitalist upstairs has long been a kind of aristocracy that concentrates wealth and power in itself and its heirs, carrying a strong residue of feudal and absolutist influence rendering the downstairs far less empowered than democratic ideals would suggest.[17]

As shown earlier, the capitalist aristocracy upstairs have long crafted their own Security story with strong feudal and absolutist elements to win over its "plain folk" downstairs. Moreover, the capitalist Security story, as in feudalism, is an emotionally resonant narrative, playing off of eternally powerful and mysterious experiences of enemies, fear and protection. As we shall see, the capitalist modern story is an offspring in new guise of much of the feudal story—surprising because we think of modern democracy as transcending all the evil, absolutist or arbitrary authority relations of the ancient world.

The medieval feudal world was made up of baronies or principalities ruled by aristocrats before kings and queens consolidated larger sovereign nation states in the absolutist era. Each feudal barony was composed of one or many "manors," estates ruled by the lords—who were often Church officials—that constituted the major economic feudal unit. Marc Bloch, the great historian of medieval feudal society, described the manor as follows:

A manor was first and foremost an estate . . . but an estate inhabited by the lord's subjects. As a rule, the area thus delimited was in
its turn divided into two closely interdependent parts. On the one
hand, there was the "demesne" . . . all the produce of which was
taken directly by the lord; on the other there were the tenements,
or medium sized peasant holdings, which, in varying numbers,
were grouped around the lord's "court."[18]

As Bloch notes:

The principal object of the powers enjoyed by the chief(or lord)
was to provide him with revenue by securing for him a portion of
the produce of the soil . . . the superior power which the lord pos-
sessed was . . . above all, the right to impose taxes and demand services. The latter consisted for the most part in agricultural labour
services performed on the demesne. Thus, at least at the beginning
of the feudal era, when these compulsory labour services were particularly heavy, the tenements not only added their contribution in
produce or money to the revenues of the fields directly exploited
by the master; they were in addition a source of manpower in the
absence of which those fields must have lain fallow.[19]

The lord supervised all production—essentially the "boss" in modern parlance—and also held strict political and judicial control. He had
powers of taxation and imprisonment. He had the right to appropriate
lands when serfs died without heirs, and controlled courts, able to thus
personally decide any conflicts on the manor, an early form of absolutism and also appearing in new dress in modern fascist and authoritarian
capitalist societies in Europe and the US.

The manor was the upstairs/downstairs medieval feudal house. The
lords lived upstairs in "courts" with large land holdings reserved just for
themselves, while the downstairs was occupied by peasants who had
small homes and land plots on the lord's great estate. The manor was an
early paradigm of the extreme inequality that is the headliner of today's
capitalist economies.

But unlike today, the feudal "houses" or manors made no pretense of equality or democracy. The lord ran the house and fused in his own person both economic control and political power, a kind of power separated legally in modern capitalist democracies. The power of the lord was often depicted approvingly in ways that evoke the tyranny of a slave-holder:

> he is mine from the soles of his feet to the crown of his head, an abbot of Vezalay said of one of his serfs.[20]

Medieval serfs lived in eternal bondage to this concentrated lordly power. There was virtually no possibility of social mobility and no aspiration for it. There was no stairway to climb in this feudal house, nor was there any reason for it, since both lords and serfs could barely imagine either the prospect or desirability of a more equal order.

As the social theorist and historian, Erich Fromm, put it:

> Everybody in the earlier period was chained to his role in the social order. A man had little chance to move socially from one class to another, he was hardly able to move even geographically from one town or from one country to another. With few exceptions he had to stay where he was born.[21]

The serf's bondage did come with a certain form of life-long commitment that the capitalist wage worker does not enjoy. The medieval lord could not "fire" the serf, though he could kill him for disobedience. The entire downstairs/upstairs order—based on unquestioned authority and submission and the lack of freedom to change one's station in life—was ordained by God or nature and was not subject to rational analysis or questioning.

Feudalism was a society of deep dependency in which every relation expressed an unbreakable bond of an inferior serving his superior. Bloch explains it through an iconic image that came to represent feudal society:

> Imagine two men face to face; one wishing to serve, the other willing or anxious to be served. The former puts his hands together and places them, thus joined between the hand of the other man—a plain

symbol of submission, the significance of which was sometimes further emphasized by a kneeling posture.[22]

Bloch shows how this became a defining image of medieval feudal life:

> Described or mentioned in the texts a hundred times, reproduced on seals, miniatures, bas-reliefs, the ceremony (of submission through kneeling) was called "homage". . . . The superior person, whose position was created by this act, was described by no other term than the very general one of "lord". Similarly, the subordinate was often simply called the "man" of this lord.[23]

Bloch notes that this relation of "homage" defined the heart of feudalism as a social order, and lower lords had a relation to higher lords; subordination was across the board:

> The emphasis was on the fundamental element in common across all feudal relations: the subordination of one individual to another.[24]

Bloch explains that this dependency and subordination developed in their earliest feudal forms in the 8th and 9th centuries. At first, they had no direct religious foundation in Christianity. But as feudal society developed into a more crystallized theological order, homage and all feudal relations of submission in the feudal house assumed a more explicitly Godly form, as religious rites were added to the homage ceremony:

> homage in due course ceased to be acceptable to a society which had come to regard a promise as scarcely valid unless God were guarantor . . . a second rite—an essentially religious one—was superimposed on it; laying his hand on the Gospels or on relics, the vassal (or kneeling man) swore to be faithful to his master. This was called fealty.[25]

In the evolving feudal order, the aristocrats had a grace given to them by God and nature. They were guardians within the "Great Chain of

Being," grounded in tradition, in which everyone was interconnected but had an assigned place. The defining image of kneeling—or a lower lord to a higher one, or the more brutal slave-like subordination of the serf—affirmed not just a secular political authority but a God that reaffirmed the righteousness of the upstairs-downstairs feudal order and conveyed a measure of honor and respect to all who accepted it, even the lowliest serf. This all-powerful Godly form of feudal authority was passed on to the absolutist-era monarchs, symbolized by Louis XIV who proclaimed "the state is me"—and has been reclaimed today by authoritarian leaders such as Donald Trump who pronounced at the Republican National Convention:

I am your voice. I alone can fix it. I will restore law and order.[26]

The lords were known as "blue bloods"—a term that some felt developed to describe the beautiful blue veins on pure white aristocratic skin that could not be seen on serfs. Whether that is true or not, it reflects a key part of the medieval Security story: that the upstairs was by God, as well as by history and social norms, permanently superior to the downstairs. The differences created an enduring and blessed chasm between the lords and serfs because the "essence" of the lord and his serfs was so different. The lord is an upstairs caste and the serf a downstairs caste. But the serf gained a certain honor by being connected, if totally subordinated to the lord. In the glory of subordination to the lord, the serf also gained a certain glory.

Caste divisions are different than class differences.[27] In the Meritocracy, people in lower capitalist classes can move up through hard work and talent into a higher class—and earn the right to live upstairs and the power to protect the downstairs. But since feudalism is built on caste rather than class identity, the Meritocracy story is nonsensical. The whole notion of caste is that the inherited nature or essence of the aristocrats and serfs is different, and that no effort or hard work can ever turn the lower caste into a higher caste. While this is drastically different from modern capitalist democratic and egalitarian ideals, remember that the 1% upstairs today is resurfacing as its own form of aristocracy or caste, and that our capitalist classes are becoming more like medieval castes, where you live your entire life in more or less the same station as your parents.[28]

The general culture that prevailed in pre-capitalist social systems, as noted by the philosopher, Karl Mannheim, assumed that:

> Men are essentially unequal, unequal in their gifts and abilities, and unequal in the core of their being.[29]

Feudal culture and the absolutist era that followed both fit this bill perfectly, with an upstairs/downstairs social and political order of castes. Mannheim wrote that:

> In pre-democratic society, all social authority is inextricably linked to the idea of the ontological superiority of the wielder of authority. No person, family or institution can exert authority without being regarded as made of "higher" stuff than the ordinary run of humanity.[30]

These pervasive cultural beliefs about the virtues of inequality have echoes today in capitalist narratives that the cream rises to the top—with the upstairs reflecting people superior in talent and merit. Even if the upstairs is a divinely blessed caste, feudalism nonetheless needed a robust legitimating story to sustain its own extreme upstairs/downstairs order. A super-predatory lord, who taxed or abused too much, or a crop failure, or natural disasters could create unbearable suffering or havoc. Serfs in theory could unite against the lords in their manor—or with other serfs in neighboring feudal manors against the whole feudal order. Such revolts were relatively rare, but only because the legitimating story operated with such great mystical force that it seemed invisible and unnecessary.

True, the idea that upstairs was divinely ordained to rule created its own immensely powerful legitimacy, especially in a world defined by God and religion. If the upstairs has been chosen by God to rule, a crisis of legitimacy would have to come, it seems, from a crisis in religious faith. And while doubt in God exists in all eras, it was not widespread in the deeply religious Middle Ages.

Nonetheless, the original foundations of feudalism—and the belief in the legitimacy of the serf subordinated to his lord, was based on an idea not just of divine authority but divine—and earthly—responsibility. Bloch makes clear that the power of the lord over his serfs was accepted because it came with responsibilities to him. The feudal concept of subordination of the downstairs could only be sustained legitimately if the upstairs delivered on a truly great responsibility: to provide security against a vast range of threats, both real and invented by the lord and medieval culture.

The Security story of the Middle Ages was a protection pact of both physical and spiritual security. At the heart of the feudal world and Security story is the idea that their superior nature obliges aristocrats to protect those incapable of protecting themselves, a notion also reappearing in the Security story of early and contemporary capitalism, where it resurfaces today in sacred concepts such as "national security" guaranteed by our own knights or warriors of honor in the Pentagon.

Bloch makes clear that the relation of lord to serf was all about protection. The aristocrats had inherited and created a world of fear that overwhelmed the downstairs. In Bloch's telling, the feudal manor—and the ceremonial homage of kneeling and submission that symbolized the essence of the feudal house itself—was a story and "deal" crafted by the upstairs to offer security and protection to a frightened, even terrified, population.

> Everywhere the weak man felt the need to be sheltered by someone more powerful. The powerful man, in his turn, could not maintain his prestige or his fortune or even ensure his own safety except by securing for himself, by persuasion or coercion, the support of subordinates bound to his service.[31]

The quest for protection—central to any Security story—was so strong in feudal society that not just the weakest and poorest, but free people and even lower and some higher lords accepted submission to superiors as necessary for their survival and well-being.

Among the lowly people who sought a protector the most unfortunate became simply slaves, thereby binding their descendants as well as themselves. Many others, however, even among the most humble, were eager to maintain their status as free men; and the persons who received their allegiance had as a rule little reason to oppose such a wish.[32]

Elites presiding over great inequality in any era turn to the Security story to justify their rule in the name of the most primitive and emotionally compelling desire: survival. There are always real economic, social and military threats than can create an emotionally resonant Security story. But in feudalism, capitalism and other upstairs/downstairs societies, elites make their Security stories more compelling by constructing on top of real threats a hierarchy of new threats—a material and spiritual world that is populated by enemies they invent or manufacture or inflate.

To understand the emotional power of protection of the feudal Security story, remember that the Middle Ages were also known as the Dark Ages. It was a world of perpetual fear. There were very real constant threats to survival: epidemics, famine and violence, though some of these threats came from the lords' control over money, land and services that could ward off disease and poverty from themselves. But there were also all the threats created by the theological worldview; these were also partially invented or purveyed by clerical and landed elites who conceived existence as pervaded by Satan and evil enemies. Bloch writes of a torrent of wild emotionalism in a religious culture dominated by extreme irrationality, leading to:

an astonishing sensibility to what were believed to be supernatural manifestations. It made people's minds constantly and almost morbidly attentive to all manner of signs, dreams or hallucinations . . . the influence of mortifications of the flesh and the repression of natural instincts joined to that of a mental attitude . . . centered on the problems of the unseen. No psychoanalyst has ever examined dreams more earnestly than the monks of the tenth

or the eleventh centuries. Yet the laity also shared the emotionalism of a civilization in which moral or social convention did
not yet require well-bred people to repress their tears and their
raptures. The despairs, the rages, the impulsive acts, the sudden
revulsions of feelings present great difficulties to historians, who
are instinctively disposed to reconstruct the past in terms of the
rational. But the irrational is an important element in all history
and only a sort of false shame could allow its effects on the course
of political events in feudal Europe to be passed over in silence.[33]

Of course, the same could be said today, where the capitalist claim to
rationality has led us now to once again "pass over" the many elements
of contemporary irrationality and its effects on our politics. But our
Halloween costumes remind us today of that feudal fear, scaring kids
with ghosts and devils and evil spirits all part of the medieval world.
Bloch elaborates:

> waves of fear swept almost incessantly over this region or that,
> subsiding at one point only to rise again elsewhere. Sometimes a
> vision started the panic. Or perhaps a great historic calamity like
> the destruction of the Holy Sepulchre in 1009, or again perhaps
> merely a violent tempest.[34]

There were violent bandits, diseases and evil spirits—all faces of
Satan—invading every part of medieval life. To live in that era of Satan
meant to be horribly afraid much of your life, even though faith in God
provided believers with reassurances of divine security. Bloch fills his
history with portraits of a religious culture steeped in fear, one partly
crafted and "managed" by the most powerful clergy and lords:

> Below the One God and subordinated to his Almighty Power . . .
> mankind imagined the opposing wills of a host of beings good and
> bad in a state of perpetual strife; saints, angels and especially dev-
> ils. "Who does not know", wrote the priest Helmold that the wars,
> the mighty tempests the pestilences, all the ills, indeed that inflict
> the human race, occur through the agency of demons?[35]

It is thus hardly surprising that a Security story promising safety and spiritual as well as material protection could create strong emotional resonance, and that extreme inequality might even be welcomed by the medieval downstairs. An ordinary serf would be desperate—and grateful—for an all-powerful authority figure. It would be important that the lord of the manor be extremely strong, even if brutal and a threat to you if you displeased him. Because such an all-powerful ruler would surely have the power to destroy one's enemies and provide protection in an irrational and frightening world full of evil spirits. The emotional appeal of "strongmen" rulers in today's capitalist world, also now full of real and invented enemies, is one of the feudal legacies we see resurfacing with a vengeance in the modern age.

The feudal Security story was a credible promise of protection against all the satanic forces. The aristocrats might be cruelly exploitative and monopolize power and wealth. But they promised a relatively safe and stable place in the manor to poor and frightened people. And as for their Security story, a lifetime protection pact, it is easy to see its attraction. Serfs were assured tenure within the manor on their land, and could not be thrown out to be eaten by the wolves, killed by roving bandits or consumed in the wilds by devils.

The lords, after all, were mainly warriors of God, who embodied a culture of military honor and divinely inspired valor. No other caste could contest them on the battlefield, whether physical or spiritual.

The lords of the manor thus defended turf against very real enemies: other rival lords, from near or afar, who might try to conquer the land and rape or kill the serfs. The enemy could be the noble on the next manor, who was often a relative, or it could be distant heathen Moslems, who had seized the Holy Lands in Palestine from God's chosen Christians. The feudal world was also full of roving bandits, another constant threat the lords could repel from the manor.

Beyond such "manor security," analogous to the modern religion of national security, the lords provided spiritual security. As vessels or instruments of God, they had powers to defend serfs against many satanic enemies, both real and imagined. These included threats of the evil eye and of God's wrath, whether disease or deadly storms, in any form. To be protected by the lord of the manor was to be at one with the Lord of the universe—and thus to gain the honor of a house and instrument of God.

As shown in the next chapter, the defense against real or invented enemies is a core part of the capitalist Security story—which also assures safety and protection in a threatening world. But there is yet another element of the feudal Security story that surfaces in today's Security story. It involves the construction of a medieval form of tribalism or "nationalism," that gave ordinary people a sense of community and honor.

Such collective identity was built into the blood and land of the feudal manor. The manor was an enduring refuge and home, with all serfs knowing that they would always "belong" to the manor and work their same plot of land, as their ancestors did and their children and children's children would. The manor—and the larger feudal society it undergirded—was thus a "way of life" that lived on across many generations, and gave a moral and honorable identity to serfs who were virtually slaves but part of what we might now call the tribe or nation.

One of the great human fears is isolation, being cut off from a community that knows and protects you. The manor and all the feudal deep relations of subordination offered that community, an anchor that extorted and suppressed but also protected serfs from becoming refuse in the wilds.

The manor's community honor or pride—what we might call "patriotism" today—came from the honor of its reigning lord. The lord of the manor was the living symbol uniting everyone—upstairs and downstairs—in the feudal tribe or nation. Because of his "blue blood," everyone knew that God had blessed this manor, since the blood in the lord's veins came from a blessed and higher power. Serfs with no power whatsoever gained a certain glory through their protection from their lord and their belonging to a divine-blessed manor and noble. It is hardly surprising that capitalist tycoons have aped or imitated ancient aristocrats, building their great houses in Newport or their lavish clothes and furnishings modeled after kings, queens and lords of the greatest manors. Capitalism rhetorically rejects the politics of blood, but in practice capitalists have always tried to define themselves as blue bloods themselves, since there is no more potent way of legitimating one's essence as rightful ruler of the world and uniting any upstairs with its downstairs, while also vesting the downstairs with reflected glory.

3

TRUMP-ING FREEDOM
FOR PROTECTION

HOW TO WIN FRIENDS BY
MANUFACTURING ENEMIES

Donald Trump yells: "I am your voice. I alone can fix it. I will restore law and order."

Convention Delegates shout back: "USA! Lock her up! Build the Wall! Trump!"

—National Republican Convention, July 2016

Take up the White Man's burden
In patience to abide
To veil the threat of terror
And check the show of pride

—Rudyard Kipling, 1899

We are 9/11 babies.

—Our students, 2018

Donald Trump was never shy about announcing that he would be a security president whose biggest job was to protect the nation. At the 2016 Republican National Convention, he pronounced the core rhetorical flourish of all Security stories:

The most basic duty of government is to defend the lives of its own citizens. Any government that fails to do so is a government unworthy to lead.[1]

Trump went on to say in his acceptance speech:

Our convention occurs at a moment of crisis for our nation. The attacks on our police, and the terrorism in our cities, threaten our very way of life. Any politician who does not grasp this danger is not fit to lead our country.

Americans watching this address tonight have seen the recent images of violence in our streets and the chaos in our communities. Many have witnessed this violence personally. Some have even been its victims.

I have a message for all of you: The crime and violence that today afflicts our nation will soon—and I mean very soon come to an end. Beginning on January 20th 2017, safety will be restored.[2]

By the end of his first year as President, Donald Trump had tweeted about a world full of enemies out to destroy America, undermine its great economy and cultural heritage, and kill American citizens. He alone would solve it, laying out the foundations of his Security story that would dominate his presidency. *Much of his tale was told earlier by both Republican and Democratic presidents—so it is a long and deep part of the American national religion of national security.*

Trump's version is full of bigotry and authoritarian dangers, but it is also laced with economic populism, some of which reinforces the critique of capitalism and its global crisis that Leftists have long spotlighted. The Security story of Republicans since Reagan has increasingly drawn white workers with real grievances, and thus the entire story needs to be understood as something more complex than simply racism, sexism or authoritarianism, though it is, indeed, all these things.

The bigotry of Trump's Security story was clear in the enemies that he ranted about from the beginning of his campaign. Some were

Mexican immigrants surging at and across the border he called "rapists" and "dealing drugs." These included the members of the Salvadoran violent gang, MS-13. He told a White House meeting:

> You wouldn't believe how bad these people are. These aren't people, these are ANIMALS.[3]

There were also the "radical Islamic terrorists," Muslims who he had promised to call out by their religion. ISIS and Al Qaeda were just the tip of the iceberg of Islamic terror nations or groups such as Iran, Hamas, Hezballoh, the Afghan Taliban, the Nigerian Boka Haram— just a smattering of the terrorists on all continents and inside the US itself. In his Inaugural address, Trump vowed to eliminate them all, saying he would lead the battle:

> against Radical Islamic Terrorism, which we will eradicate completely from the face of the Earth.[4]

Trump was tweeting a great deal about domestic enemies as well as foreign ones. They included Blacks, especially young men who terrorized the streets, other lazy or violent Black people looking for government handouts and draining the taxpayers' money, and activists such as Black Lives Matter thugs who disrespected or killed police. Trump said on July 2016 in his speech at the Republican National Convention:

> The attacks on our police, and the terrorism in our cities, threaten our very way of life. Any politician who does not grasp this danger is not fit to lead our country.[5]

There were also all the anti-American protesters at his rallies, the ones he urged his supporters to "rough up" and "throw out." At one rally in 2016, he had security guards physically push out a Black man who shouted "Black Lives Matter." Trump shouted back:

> Get him the hell out of here.[6]

This led several Trump supporters to attack the man, shoving, tackling and kicking him with Trump looking on. In fact, Trump told his admirers:

> Knock the crap out of them, would you? Just knock the hell—I will pay any legal fees. I promise. I promise.[7]

Trump went after many other enemies who looked respectable but were just as dangerous: the "fake news" media, the liberals who took over Hollywood, the civil servants in the "deep state," the anti-constitutional liberal judges, the federal "witch-hunters" investigating him in the Mueller probe, the politically correct professors corrupting students and the universities, the anti-Second Amendment activists who want to "take away your guns," the liberal social workers and other members of the social welfare government who want to tax you to feed their shiftless clients and pad their own government salaries and perks. And not least, by any means, were the enemy he called the liberal "globalists," the liberal political Establishment, who were mis-managing the economy and selling out the American worker:

> The political establishment that is trying to stop us is the same group responsible for our disastrous trade deals, massive illegal immigration and economic and foreign policies that have bled our country dry. The political establishment has brought about the destruction of our factories and our jobs as they flee to Mexico, China and other countries all around the world. It's a global power structure that is responsible for the economic decisions that have robbed our working class, stripped our country of its wealth and put that money into the pockets of a handful of large corporations and political entities.[8]

Trump's Security story thus included destroying upstairs enemies, *incorporating a populist tone that spoke to real economic grievances of working Americans and gave his story special power*, a theme we noted earlier and need to return to frequently. As the progressive social critic, Thomas

Frank observes, Trump actually incorporates a good deal of the Left critique of neo-liberal "free trade" and of global capitalism in his Right-wing populism. Frank writes that:

> In each of the speeches I watched, Trump spent a good part of his time talking about an entirely legitimate issue, one that could even be called leftwing.

> Yes, Donald Trump talked about trade. In fact, to judge by how much time he spent talking about it, trade may be his single biggest concern—not white supremacy. Not even his plan to build a wall along the Mexican border, the issue that first won him political fame. He did it again during the debate on 3 March: asked about his political excommunication by Mitt Romney, he chose to pivot and talk about . . . trade.

> It seems to obsess him: the destructive free-trade deals our leaders have made, the many companies that have moved their production facilities to other lands, the phone calls he will make to those companies' CEOs in order to threaten them with steep tariffs unless they move back to the US.[9]

Frank notes that empirical studies show that Trump voters "are much more frightened than they are bigoted."[10] Frank cites a Working America study of 1,600 Trump voters, which

> confirmed what we heard all the time: people are fed up, people are hurting, they are very distressed about the fact that their kids don't have a future . . . there still hasn't been a recovery from the recession, that every family still suffers from it in one way or another.[11]

Trump's Security story includes a promise to protect working Americans against some of the very enemies and capitalist ills—particularly trade and outsourcing of jobs—that liberals and the Left have focused on for years. His security narrative thus resonates partly because it speaks *on the economic front* to such crucial real problems of US workers—and there is an overlap between Trump's story and the very Left that reviles him and he reviles.

Nonetheless, while Trump's Security story taps into deep economic anxieties of US workers, his solutions will make things far worse. His Security story is a fervent defense of capitalism and the rich, as well as an extreme polemical argument against liberals and the Left, while targeting, as seen, people of color, immigrants and others in the basement. Trumpist policies—including his tax cuts for the rich, cuts in health care and education, and anti-union militancy devastated rather than helped the downstairs he claimed he would protect at all costs.

Trump signaled dangerous authoritarianism in the ways he attacked his opponents. He savaged the "bi-coastal elites" and liberal Democrats he claims actually run the "rigged" Establishment, promising to investigate and likely put behind bars the criminal Hillary Clinton. Chants of "Lock her up; lock her up, lock her up" rippled across his rallies. This could resonate in parts of the American downstairs, as we shall see, not just because of authoritarian tendencies among Evangelicals and some conservative workers but because many leading Democrats, including both Bill and Hillary Clinton, were not advancing policies that would truly lift the American worker—and that, indeed disrespected many of the "forgotten people."

Trump's Security story led him to call even centrist or mainstream Democrats enemies of the nation, with many workers agreeing because Democratic Administrations since Reagan had abandoned much of the New Deal and failed to protect economic security of working people of any race, while also failing to address the cultural anxieties of white working Americans. Speaking on February 5, 2018, Trump said this of the Democrats who did not stand up and clap for him at his State of the Union Address, remaining in their seats:

> they were like death, and un-American, un-American. Somebody said treasonous, I mean, yeah I guess, why not? Can we call that treason, why not?[12]

All these enemies were lead actors in Trump's Security story—which was a logical, if surreal, elaboration of the Security story bred since 1980 in the Reagan revolution. Security stories are always narratives about how upstairs elites in different eras seek to win over the downstairs by crushing enemies of the nation, protecting ordinary people from a fantastic and frightening array of enemies, that, as in Trump's story, can include liberal economic and political elites actually in the American upstairs and the mezzanine, while actually incorporating some liberal ideas. Trump's enemy list was portrayed in a flamboyant and super-murderous plot that might have come out of a Stephen King novel. But it spoke emotionally to many white folk downstairs that had, indeed, been abandoned, and made them open to and even hungry for the broader Security story Trump was pedaling.

Much of the Trump story has roots cultivated even before Reagan. Corporate elites in the early 1970s funded "The New Right" with an early version of the Trump Security story to ward off the Martin Luther Kings, the student anti-war activists, the environmentalists, the feminists, the anti-poverty crusaders and other activists of the 1960s; all these Leftist traitors would be used to rally the "moral majority," the real Americans who would follow Trump to save their jobs and their "tribe" or nation even if "I shot somebody on Fifth Avenue."

Trump's enemies were thus his prop "apprentices" in his new very real political Reality Show, who would get fired at by military and police, as well as fired by the big companies and banks. The new enemies were part of a deadly serious new Security story that was not just entertainment but a narrative of how to run the country. Working people downstairs would look to Trump and his fellow 1% to protect their jobs, their culture and their physical safety and survival against threats never seen at such horrific and frightening levels. In the end, it was all about protection of a frightened people!

Walls, Nukes and God: Trump as Protector

The role of the enemies as lead characters in Trump's Security story came out early in his political campaign, which had one clear agenda: crush and destroy America's enemies. He would use every instrument possible—from the military to divine intervention—to protect Americans against all its fearsome enemies.

Trump's Republican supporters highlighted his selection by God:

> "God raised up, I believe, Donald Trump" said former US Rep. Michele Bachmann after he won the GOP nomination. "God showed up," the Rev. Franklin Graham said to cheers at a post-election rally. . . . "For me, that has to be providence. That has to be the hand of God," said Paula White, an evangelical pastor Trump has tapped to pray at his inauguration.[13]

The leading symbol of Trump's protection story was the Wall:

> We're going to build a wall folks, don't worry, we're going to build a wall. That wall will go up so fast, your heads will spin. And you'll say, "you know, know he meant it!" And you know what else I mean? Mexico is going to pay for the wall.[14]

What better than a Wall to be the headliner of a Security story, a Wall that would keep out the enemies and keep America safe. It would be a "big, beautiful" Wall, locking out all the Muslims, terrorists, immigrants and other foreign enemies threatening our heritage.

Of course, along with the Wall, he would keep out Muslims by issuing travel bans against Muslin nations, another symbol of protection above all else, even if it meant ending America's history of endless immigration.

There was also the promise of an all-out war on global terrorism, with nuclear weapons that would be used whenever necessary. Trump told Bloomberg News he wanted to be "unpredictable" about using nukes against ISIS and said:

> "I'm never going to rule anything out" (about using nuclear weapons as first strike battlefield weapons).[15]

To defend the nation against its internal enemies, Trump promised more internal "Walls": more prisons and police and guns and law-and-order justices. In his Inaugural Address, he made clear he would end "American carnage":

> the crime and gangs and drugs that have stolen too many lives and robbed our country of so much unrealized potential. . . . This American carnage stops right here and stops right now.[16]

There would be a new Supreme Court that would ensure at the highest level that the domestic enemies would be locked up for a long time—especially the Blacks and Browns running amok in American cities. But Trump promised also to destroy their liberal patrons in the socialist social welfare state and their allies in activist circles. The Trump security policy would "drain the swamp" of the liberal "deep state," the politically correct welfare bureaucracies, and the socialist PC universities and mass media who were feeding themselves and their client underclass, thereby undermining the safety and prosperity of the nation.

Trump's enemies were enumerated to make sure his Security story was loud and clear. I—and I alone—will protect the true American heroes: the military, the veterans, the police, the small town business men and farmers, the Rust Belt workers, the white Evangelicals, all the "forgotten people." In his Inaugural Address, he proclaimed:

> The forgotten men and women of our country will be forgotten no longer. Everyone is listening to you now. . . . From this moment on, it's going to be America First. . . . We must protect our borders from the ravages of other countries making our products, stealing our companies and destroying our jobs. Protection will lead to great prosperity and strength. . . . We will be protected by the great men and women of our military and law enforcement and, most importantly, we are protected by God.[17]

Trump was offering a Security story based on *protection*—the word he repeated over and over again in his Inaugural. He offered true Americans all forms of protection: economic, cultural and physical protection. "Make America Great Again," the concluding words of his Inaugural, were a protection pact especially for the forgotten people: securing their jobs and protecting their great American Christian heritage. In his Inaugural, he highlighted protecting jobs in his anti-globalist and nationalist protection story:

> We will bring back our jobs. We will bring back our borders. We will bring back our wealth. And we will bring back our dreams.[18]

And he also promised the cultural protection of bringing back Christmas and celebrating traditional American religion and cultural heritage:

> end the war on Christmas. . . . We can say Merry Christmas again.[19]

This was all part of restoring and protecting the forgotten people's rightful place as True Americans; they would once again be protected, respected and honored. His message: your enemies—all those attacking your hard work, your religion, your politically incorrect beliefs and your "deplorable" American traditions—are my enemies and will be forever destroyed. My Presidency is your protection!

The Trump Security story—whose basic plot and "protection pact" goes all the way back to medieval feudalism—is not new in America. It features two types of enemies—foreign and domestic. Trump won because he convinced the country that destroying these enemies would save the nation.

Enemies in All Security Stories: Ten Generalities

Before discussing in more detail the two main types of enemies in Trump's Security story, we need to make a few points about enemies that are characteristic of almost all Security stories and put them in proper context.

- First, some enemies are real. The world has always been dangerous and every nation and person faces threats. It is the reality of enemies and survival threats that gives the Security story its credibility and power. In recent history, Nazi Germany was a real enemy. Today, cyber threats against our grid and communications system are a true threat. The greatest authentic enemies include deadly diseases and hurricanes, floods and droughts, many brought on by climate change, the most overwhelmingly important real enemy. Ignoring enemies such as climate change and nuclear war helps presidents craft their Security story by displacing subliminal fears of extreme real threats to other enemies they manufacture.

- Second, the Security story "hypes" enemies, gaining believers or follow-ers who are literally scared "out of their minds" by the exaggerations. The exaggeration of the Soviet Threat by American presidents—both Republican and Democratic—during the Cold War is an obvious example.

- Third, the nation's own leaders create many of their enemies by their own policies. US invasions or wars, for example, created enemies of nations, such as Iran, which was an ally prior to the CIA's overthrow of the Iranian president Mohammed Mossadegh in 1953. The US elites then treat Iran as a real enemy when they have converted it into one—in a sense, a half-real and half-invented enemy.

- Fourth, many enemies that get top billing in the Security story are not real at all. They are completely invented or "manufactured." The existence of real threats makes it possible to manufacture enemies that people fear, transferring fear of real enemies to invented ones. The fear of more violent criminals is invented today, as violent crime rates are going down, but they feed the fear of minority, immigrant and poor groups who the upstairs likes to designate as criminals.

- Fifth, certain key real enemies and security threats are always ignored in leading Security stories. Climate change is purged from Trump's National Security story. A nation's greatest enemies are often its ruling elites, but the Security story will never identify them because they craft the story. The threat to America now centrally involves the destruction of its democracy by billionaire elites more committed to their hedge funds and profits than to the Constitu-tion, but the capitalist upstairs will never offer a Security story that describes the 1% as the enemy.

- Sixth, domestic enemies are as important or more important than foreign enemies in many Security stories. Such "fifth columns" or internal enemies are often the main ones because they can be portrayed as imposters who are not true members of the nation or tribe. The Security story always spotlights domestic enemies—today, illegal immigrants or Black Americans or American Muslims—because, when purged, they rally the "true" tribe downstairs to join the upstairs. Security stories typically "work" in this tribal fashion, dividing the downstairs against each other rather than against elites. Hitler chose enemies—Jews, Slavs, gypsies—who he could exterminate and thereby rally the true Aryan German race around him (his "base" as we would say today). Disgraced enemies build the power, honor and self-respect that downstairs people crave.

- Seventh, no Security story wins the support of everyone—whether in the upstairs or the downstairs. For example, Trump's Security story is rejected by the great majority of people of color downstairs and upstairs, by the majority of women, by young people and, in fact, the majority of the country. The same was true of Hitler, who never got more than about 40% of the vote before he abolished elections. Security stories can propel leaders to power simply by mobilizing a highly emotionally charged and activist base, even if it is a minority in the nation.

- Eighth, the purpose of all Security stories is to maintain the power of elites living upstairs by winning the heart of the downstairs. They craft "enemy stories" most likely to win emotional resonance of declining people downstairs, even if either the story or enemy might contradict some of their own values. The Trump Security story was rejected by some of the capitalist elites upstairs because it is anti-Cosmopolitan and appeals to the traditionalism of the white people downstairs. Thus, not only do many downstairs folks reject the Trump Security story but so do many capitalist elites upstairs, as in the case of ABC firing Trump's fan Roseanne Barr for racist tweets consistent with Trump's security story but not with that of Disney, the parent company of ABC.

- Ninth, the Security story is only one of multiple legitimating stories. Indeed there are even multiple versions of today's American Security story itself. As the Meritocracy story weakens, different US elites lean more heavily on their own version of the Security Story. There are serious divisions upstairs as well as downstairs about competing legitimating narratives.

- Tenth, one of the multiple legitimating stories, particularly in capitalism, is the idea of TINA—or There is No Alternative. Capitalism may be creating awful inequality and declining mobility, but it is still the only economy that can create mass prosperity. Sometimes that economy can be mis-managed in ways that don't spread benefits to all the people downstairs; Trump's stories made a very big argument that liberal "globalists" had promoted an economic agenda that has hurt American working people and many American small and large businesses. These globalist thinkers and leaders are also enemies, distorting the promise and unique ability of capitalism to create prosperity for everyone. So, along with the Security story—or as part of it in Trump's case—is a legitimating story that capitalism, properly managed by smart deal-makers and protected against the enemies of the common worker downstairs, will always lead to the best standard of living for the downstairs. TINA!

TINA—as just discussed—points to a major caveat in discussing Trump's political story. In looking at Trump's Security story, and his overall political appeal, there is one broader point that needs to be highlighted. While the Security story is a very big part of Trump's appeal—and has long been part of capitalist legitimating strategies, Trump launched a populist *economic* appeal to the "forgotten people" that promised new trade policies, tax cuts and jobs for the downstairs working class. Trump promised to be the voice of the real American heroes: the great American working class:

> Every day I wake up determined to deliver for the people I have met all across this nation that have been neglected, ignored, and abandoned. I have visited the laid-off factory workers, and the

communities crushed by our horrible and unfair trade deals. These are the forgotten men and women of our country, and they are forgotten, but they're not going to be forgotten long. These are people who work hard but no longer have a voice. I AM YOUR VOICE.[20]

This part of Trump's Security story is crucial to be remembered, because it points to the only way to counter it. The sense of vulnerability—to physical danger and survival—that gives emotional power to the Security story is deeply rooted in the failures of Democrats, liberals and the Left to become a real "voice" for much of the working people downstairs. And the only way to offer a different and more humane story—that can emotionally draw the American downstairs from Trumpism and the conservative Right to a progressive politics—is to build a progressive movement and Democratic politics that truly does what Trump promised but will never do: actually restore the economic and cultural well-being of the American downstairs.

Enemy 1—The Foreign Enemy

Our students describe themselves as "9/11" babies. By that, they mean that the attacks on the Twin Towers were the defining event of their political consciousness. Elites know this—and realized the attacks were a gift. They couldn't have dreamed up a better group of enemies to build the 21st-century version of the Security story.

Every Security story needs an "umbrella enemy." The umbrella enemy is the most dangerous and frightening foreign foe threatening the nation. It creates the fear that will always bind the downstairs to the upstairs, and it keeps the faith in the religion of "national security" that is worshipped by downstairs and upstairs alike.

Terrorism has long been one of the umbrella enemies, used by almost all the European capitalist empires—Britain, France, Germany and others—to win over their own downstairs. Leaders of these empires called any movement or groups fighting against the empire terrorists. The British referred constantly to Kenyan Mau Mau fighters and other East African anti-colonial or socialist revolutionaries as terrorists. Even ancient Rome considered its primary enemy—the barbarians—to be terrorists.[21]

Terrorism replaced Communism as the umbrella enemy in the US after the Soviet empire collapsed. In some ways, terrorism is a better umbrella. The Soviet threat could always disappear if the Soviet Union disintegrated, as it did. But terrorism will never disappear. Elites can portray even small groups as dangerous terrorists because, in fact, just one or two people can do a lot of damage.

Elites have exploited the idea of terrorists for most of civilization. The ideal umbrella enemy should never be able to be destroyed. Elites can then justify building their own great institutionalized power—indeed even an Orwellian authoritarianism contrary to democratic ideals— to protect the downstairs for the long term. Orwell showed that Big Brother could only keep his dictatorial power by creating and endlessly fear-mongering about the permanent umbrella enemy—Eurasia and Eastasia.[22]

Umbrella enemies typically also create extreme visceral and personal fear. More than even large-scale war, terrorism can become a gut-level visceral focus of the population, since it can pop up in any country including the US itself. Beyond killing 3,000 people in the Twin Towers in New York and Washington DC, and blowing up passengers on a flight over Pennsylvania in the 9/11 attacks, there is always the possible terrorist next door, or the one who will blow *you* up in your favorite restaurant or sports arena. Terrorism creates anxiety about personal survival that most foreign wars don't evoke; it is specifically designed to target and kill innocent civilians who just might be you or a member of your family. It doesn't take a draft or the selective service, as in wars, to make you personally vulnerable.

Terrorism feels not only close to home but also frightening because it respects no rules, not even the rules of warfare. Images of terrorists decapitating journalists or capturing large groups of women to rape evoke the horror and, well, terror, which can bind the downstairs to the upstairs with extreme emotional intensity. Such fear not only makes ordinary people look to the upstairs for protection but willing to cede leaders great authority to win the never-ending "war on terror."

Umbrella enemies are headliners, but the Security story features many other enemies, including those who can be linked to the umbrella threat. In the US, and in much of Europe, illegal immigrants have risen almost as high as terrorists in the pantheon of enemies. When Trump called out MS-13—the Salvadoran violent gang in the US—he was manufacturing a network of Islamic terrorist, violent immigrant and domestic gang enemies that were easily melded in the public mind. Like terrorists, "aliens" such as MS-13 could strike you at home or somewhere in your local community. Trump's Attorney General, Jeff Sessions, said the MS-13's motto is "kill, rape and control." The Trump Administration claims that there are over 10,000 MS-13 members in the US and 30,000 across the world. They exaggerate the numbers and don't talk about how many of them are refugees at risk of murder at home; instead they tweet about immigration "loopholes" shown to be largely false, leading to murders of girls like Kaya Cuevas and Nisa Mickens in New York. Trump said in his 2018 State of the Union address:

> These two precious girls were brutally murdered while walking together in their hometown. . . . Many gang members have taken advantage of "glaring loopholes and our laws to enter our country as illegal unaccompanied minors."[23]

Elites exploit umbrella and linked foreign enemies to build fear and enshrine the national religion of "national security." National security is the sacred creed of the US Security story—and it binds the capitalist upstairs to everyone of the downstairs. It tells us that we need a huge and permanent military and police apparatus to protect all of us. National Security has become the core of the capitalist state, including institutions such as the CIA, FBI and Department of Justice as well as the Pentagon that sits in the middle of the Industrial-Military Complex. Veterans and police are all "heroes" because they carry out the National Security work that protects corporate profits, our own safety and the survival of the nation itself.

National Security sits at the center of the Security story and helps fuel the rise of an authoritarian model of the presidency. When enemies are looming to destroy your nation, National Security moves center stage and essentially turns the president into a full-time, unfettered Commander-in-Chief. Long before Trump, we witnessed the dramatic concentration of authority in the presidency—happening after 9/11 under George W. Bush and, even before 9/11 also under Ronald Reagan and Richard Nixon. Trump's unabashed view of himself as a king—who is not subject to the law—got much attention when he tweeted on June 4, 2018:

I have the absolute right to PARDON myself.[24]

And Trump's lawyer, Rudy Giuliani, said of Trump on June 2, 2018:

In no case, can he be subpoenaed or indicted while he's in office. No matter what it is.[25]

Even if Trump shot and killed former FBI Director James Comey, Giuliani said, Trump could not be charged with a crime because presidential authority is absolute.[26] But national security arguments have been pushing such views for years. President Nixon said in a 1977 television interview with David Frost:

Well, when the president does it, that means it is not illegal. . . . If the president, for example, approves something because of the national security . . . then the president's decision in that instance is one that enables those who carry it out, to carry it out without violating a law.[27]

Almost 50 years ago, Nixon was explicitly using the Security story to legitimate any criminal action he took in Watergate, because a president is not subject to the law. Trump nakedly displayed the ongoing shift toward an authoritarian presidency that is the most likely outcome of a society based around the Security story and National Security.

National Security is so sacred that there is no way to mount a respectable political argument that doesn't wrap itself around the flag and the honor of our National Security institutions. Interestingly, the anti-Trumpist media tried to discredit Trump by charging him with dishonoring our National Security institutions such as the FBI and

CIA. On liberal MSNBC and CNN shows every night in the Trump presidency, CIA and FBI agents or experts railed against Trump for discrediting these temples of national security. It is probably true that anti-Trumpism gets more traction or popular support if it wages war on Trump (or other Far Right leaders) arguing that he is sabotaging National Security in the name of protecting it. But it is a sad commentary that liberals need to invoke the Security story in order to discredit its most extreme proponents.

In a similar vein, Trump is attacked for cozying up to our enemies such as Russia rather than hardening our sanctions against them. Now the Russian attack on US democracy was real and profoundly serious, so it is appropriate to respond with sanctions against Russia, possible recalling of diplomats and demands for extradition of Russian intelligence officials indicted in the Mueller probe. But the "enemy story" turned anti-Trumpism into a vehicle for creating a "new Cold War," a revival of the worst phases of the old Cold War, without considering also how long-term US-backed expansion of NATO to the East toward Russian territory, as well as provocative military actions and new tactical nuke developments aimed at the Russian border are all parts of the increasingly antagonistic Russian-American relations. It is an astonishing posture for liberals and Leftists to embrace a largely one-sided view of the "new Cold War" and another mark of just how sacred the Security story is. Even liberals must prove they are good soldiers in the National Security state.

Long before Trump, both Republicans and Democrats made protecting National Security and fighting umbrella enemies their central promise. George W. Bush was the archetypical neo-conservative who represents the conservative and mostly Republican wing of the capitalist Establishment. They see the US as the "benign Empire," in the words of the leading neo-conservative writer, Max Boot, whose sacred mission is defending the world against all evil. Boot argued:

> Afghanistan and other troubled lands today cry out for the sort of enlightened foreign administration once provided by self-confident Englishmen in jodhpurs and pith helmets.[28]

And Boot approvingly quotes Rudyard Kipling's poem about the virtues of British and American imperial wars

Take up the White Man's burden—
Reap his old reward:

    The blame of those ye better
    The hate of those ye guard[29]

Like many leading neo-conservatives, Boot was an anti-Trumpist who saw Trump as insufficiently interventionist and militaristic. This was a mainstream view in the largely Republican neo-conservative establishment, whose Security story is that it is the responsibility of the US to crush all enemies of freedom and protect not just America but the entire world by putting it under US dominion.

The Democratic Establishment has long had its own Security story. Often described as "realism," this "liberal" Security story views the world of sovereign states as anarchistic, a jungle without any global government to enforce order and security. US realists, led by mostly Democratic presidents such as Bill Clinton and Barack Obama, view the role of the US to create a security blanket for itself and its allies that will protect its vital interests. This version of the Security story essentially posits all nations as enemies of each other in a realist Hobbesian world, with the US responsibility to save itself and its allies by policing the globe and maintaining balances of power ensuring US security and global order. Since all nations are potential enemies, this makes the Democratic Security story often as military interventionist as the Republican one, helping explain why President Obama surprised many by expanding military intervention and "anti-terrorist" campaigns from Afghanistan to Nigeria, presiding over the building of 700 new small military bases or "lily pads" from which the US could attack foreign enemies on every continent.[30] Obama made clear he would be relentless in using drones and special forces to kill terrorists and any American enemies:

I have made it clear that we will hunt down terrorists who threaten our country, wherever they are. That means I will not hesitate to take action against ISIL in Syria, as well as Iraq. This is a core principle of my presidency: if you threaten America, you will find no safe haven.[31]

Hillary Clinton was even more hawkish and "security-minded" than Obama. She voted in favor of the 2003 Iraq war when Obama opposed it. Clinton's warmongering and "toughness" became dogma in the Democratic Party Establishment and led the Democrats to worship the national security state every bit as much as the Republicans. The foreign enemy is a bipartisan obsession and enshrines "national security" as the national religion.

The Domestic Enemy

Many Americans are tiring of foreign wars such as Iraq and Afghanistan, wanting huge military spending to be directed back to investment in schools, health care, infrastructure and jobs at home. As noted earlier, Security stories thus posit many kinds of enemies, recognizing that the US public can become emotionally detached from foreign wars or not so worried about foreign enemies, which erodes the emotional resonance in the downstairs to the Security story. So elites have always manufactured multiple types of enemies—not just foreign ones—to ensure their Security story resonates.

Domestic enemies are always part of Security stories, and they play a key legitimating role in binding the downstairs to the upstairs. They differentiate between true members of the tribe from the imposters who threaten national security from the inside. The domestic enemies typically fragment and polarize the downstairs, part of a divide and conquer strategy in which true members of the nation living downstairs unite with the upstairs to purify the tribe and fight the imposters living on the mezzanine or in other parts of the downstairs and basement.

On May 31, 2018, Trump's National Security advisor, John Bolton, one of the most extreme neo-conservative hawks, appointed Fred Fleitz to be the NSC's executive secretary and chief of staff. Fleitz, long helping direct the Far Right Center for Security Policy (CSP), brands American Muslims, who are born here and are citizens, as inherent enemies of

America. Fleitz's CSP calls for revoking citizenship of American Muslims who follow Islamic law. CSP wrote in a 2015 report which Fleitz helped author, that the US government should:

> use shariah-adherent advocacy and practices as legal premises for deportation and stripping of American citizenship . . . must revoke the citizenship of naturalized Americans who, in seeking to insinuate shariah-compliant norms into civil society, have violated their oath of naturalization and allegiance to defend the Constitution of the United States.[32]

Trump's National Security Council top officials thus fervently argue that American Muslims are a domestic enemy, and that leading US Muslim civil society groups such as the American Muslim Brotherhood are a vital security risk. This illustrates a feature of many domestic enemies in Security stories: they are often portrayed as a fifth column (or internal enemy) tightly aligned with a leading foreign enemy, in this case Islamic groups such as Al Qaeda or ISIS waging global jihad.

Trump's attack on immigrants is another example. He created an umbrella domestic enemy of Mexican immigrants who were sweeping across the border and threating to overrun the nation and pollute its civilizational identity. Trump's 2016 campaign was a Security story stoking hatred first and foremost of the alien immigrant-as-enemy, with the border wall and harsh immigration policies to end the immigrant invasion becoming the centerpiece of his argument for being elected.

Mexican immigrants, whether refugee asylum seekers from extreme violence or undocumented workers in low-paid US agriculture jobs, exemplify the linkage of foreign enemies to domestic ones. Trump painted undocumented immigrants as such an extreme threat to the nation that they justified his "zero tolerance" policy: separating thousands of babies, toddlers and other young children from their undocumented parents who crossed the border, even as asylum seekers. Border immigration officials locked up the kids, including thousands of babies, in cages in abandoned Wal-Mart warehouses as well as military facilities.

A spokesperson for the UN human rights office condemned the US as a serious violator, saying:

> the practice of separating families amounts to arbitrary and unlawful interference in family life, and is a serious violation of the rights of the child . . . runs counter to human rights standards and principles. . . . "It is therefore of great concern that in the U.S., migration control appears to have been prioritized over the effective care and protection of migrant children. . . . Detention is never in the best interests of the child and always constitutes a child-rights violation."[33]

Much earlier, by long propagating birtherism—the idea that President Obama was a Muslim born in Kenya—a Democratic president was made a domestic enemy. It also helped link the immigrant domestic enemy not only to the foreign enemy but to other key tribal domestic enemies: both Blacks and PMC liberals (Obama was both).

The domestic enemy in the US Security story has always spotlighted race—and the idea that African-Americans are not true members of the tribe. Long before he was president, Trump was known for his racism, as when in 1991, he took out full-page ads in four New York newspapers on the "Central Park Five" story, where a group of African-Americans kids allegedly raped a white investment banker jogging in the park. Trump's ads screamed:

> Mayor Koch has stated that hate and rancor should be removed from our hearts. I do not think so. I want to hate these muggers and murderers. They should be forced to suffer and, when they kill, they should be executed for their crimes. . . . Yes, Mayor Koch, I want to hate these murderers and I always will. I am not looking to psychoanalyze or understand them, I am looking to punish them.[34]

Many years later, the kids were proved innocent after somebody else admitted raping the jogger and were freed.[35] In 2014, Trump wrote a response in an opinion piece in the *NY Daily News* saying their freeing was a "disgrace" and that

> settling doesn't mean innocence. . . . Speak to the detectives on the case and try listening to the facts. These young men do not exactly have the pasts of angels.[36]

Trump's racism is hardly a new feature of the American Security story but his dog whistle bigotry is brutal—and helps clarify the white nationalism that defines his presidency and illustrates how domestic enemies become instruments for purifying the nation and its true tribal heritage. In attacking Black athletes such as Colin Kaepernick who "took a knee" during the National Anthem, or the Black NFL Philadelphia Eagles— winners of the 2018 Super Bowl who also protested police violence at their games, Trump found a way to stigmatize African-Americans as un-American. None of the Eagles players ever "took a knee" during the entire season, but some stayed in the locker room before the game. Trump accused them of not loving the country. On June 4, 2018, he tweeted:

> Staying in the Locker Room for the playing of our National Anthem is as disrespectful to our country as kneeling.[37]

He withdrew from the Black superstar athlete winners the traditional invitation to a White House NFL celebration—and turned his action into a great celebration of America by equating their protest with lack of patriotism. By using the National Anthem as the basis of his attack on Black athletes, he was falsely representing what they did. Their actions, as the players said, had nothing to do with the Anthem. But by lying about their motives, he was able to fire up his American white base by painting Blacks as imposters who were not really members of the American tribe. As journalist Charles Blow writes,

> Donald Trump is operating the White House as a terror cell of racial grievance in America's broader culture wars. He has made his allegiances clear: He's on the side of white supremacists, white

nationalists, ethno-racists, Islamophobes and anti-Semites. He is simpatico with that cesspool.[38]

Trump's Security story is built around African-American and other enemy minorities tied to a sector of white domestic enemies. He singles out the privileged white liberals—whom we have called the PMC class living on the mezzanine of the capitalist house—who Trumpists see as conspiring with racial minorities against white workers and white Evangelical Christians. Trump here links his Security story to the emotionally visceral cultural wars polarizing the nation, as Blow notes earlier, both stoking the culture wars and using racism and fears of Black men to gain support and emotional resonance for his Security story. Trump doubled down in his rageful attacks on Black athletes who took a knee:

> Separately, on Friday night at a political rally in Alabama, Trump took to task N.F.L. players who kneel in protest during the national anthem and N.F.L. owners who *allow* it. Trump said owners should respond by saying: "Get that son of a bitch off the field right now, out, he's fired. Fired!"[39]

There is nothing new here, as all Security stories "work" by splintering the downstairs based on race, ethnicity, religion or culture. As noted earlier, Security stories are "divide and conquer" narratives, uniting a big part of the downstairs with the upstairs and turning them against other fellow downstairs inhabitants. The connection between Security stories and culture wars is explosive, and serves elite purposes by polarizing the downstairs and preventing economically disadvantaged groups from mobilizing against the upstairs. Cultural divisions trump economic ones, protecting the capitalist house from revolution by a downstairs divided in distress.

Capitalist Security stories have always exploited domestic enemies long entrenched against each other in culture wars. Trump's Security story plays off an American culture war going back to slavery, but it has its own twist. It pits the Southern and middle-of-the-country

white small town, rural folks, conservative white workers and Evangelical "*traditionalists*" against liberal urban minorities and white PMC
bi-coastal liberal globalizing elites who are "*cosmopolitans.*" As journalist
Rich Lowry writes:

> Trump is most vested in different battles, mainly against an estab-
> lishment and a north-eastern elite. . . . All during his campaign,
> he inveighed against political correctness, whose enforcers on col-
> lege campuses and in the elite culture have had the upper hand
> in establishing the agreed-upon rules for public speech. . . . His
> ongoing war with the media has to be seen through the same
> prism, as a tug of war for cultural power with an arm of the estab-
> lishment. . . . It is more tribal and raw, a cultural clash that Trump's
> team welcomes and intends to win.[40]

This "raw tribalism" has been framed around Trump's "traditionalist"
nationalism confronting global elites seeking to subordinate the US to
an international liberal world order with an alien "cosmopolitan" culture:

> Trump's nationalism is another front in this war. A nation isn't just
> a collection of people. It is a cultural expression—it has founding
> fathers, patriotic rituals and symbols, inspiring legends, traditional
> poetry and songs, a historical memory, military heroes and ceme-
> teries. In the United States, what the late political scientist Samuel
> Huntington called a "denationalised" elite has undermined these
> patriotic pillars. This elite has worked to submerge American
> sovereignty in multilateral institutions and treaties and under-
> mine its national identity through multiculturalism and mass
> immigration.[41]

Here, tribal war—what Huntington calls a "clash of civilizations"—
trumps class war, and culturally conservative workers downstairs unite
with their conservative bosses upstairs in a traditional culture and nationalism against liberal globalizing enemies both upstairs and downstairs.

Trump turns the culture wars into hostile political tribes, in which the
conservative "traditionalist" tribe is the only true American one. Trump's
Security story turns the liberal cosmopolitans and the traditionalist

workers into blood enemies. The "Red" state of mind, enthralled by Trump's Security story and his inflaming of the culture wars, views the "Blue" state of mind as culturally poisonous and the source of the ultimate threat to American civilization and survival. In the next chapter, we see that Hitler exploited his own version of this "civilization" war in the polarized German war between the "traditionalist" and nationalist Aryan countryside and the globalist cosmopolitan "Jewish" cities.

But Trump found a particularly powerful way to sell his Security story by integrating his traditionalist-cosmopolitan cultural narrative with his populist economic story. It is striking that Trump highlighted the same issues about free trade and disappearing American jobs as our most Leftist Democratic senator, Bernie Sanders, who said this:

> Not only must we fight to end disastrous unfettered free trade agreements with China, Mexico and other low wage countries, we must fight to fundamentally rewrite our trade agreements so that American products, not jobs, are our number one export.[42]

Trump thus echoed Sanders—it could be him rather than Sanders quoted above—and touched the raw nerve of the "red state" downstairs— the white "forgotten people"—by framing his Security story around both their genuine economic needs as well as their real cultural anxieties. This allowed him to inflame traditionalist white workers, conservative college-educated white Republicans and evangelical Christians as victims in a culture war with crucial economic overtones. His Security story fuels the culture wars with ugly racist and ethnic bigotry but also with rage about genuine economic oppression.

In this complex and more expansive econo-culture war that Trump intensified, his conservative "traditionalists" could fight for jobs and cultural respect, with both legitimate arguments about "being forgotten" but also ugly racism and authoritarian ideas that Trump pedaled with little reservation in his white nationalist rhetoric, famously illustrated by his comments that there were "very fine people" among the neo-Nazis and other self-declared white Nationalists marching in Charlottesville, Virginia in August, 2017. At the same time, Trump's economic populism intensified his traditionalist base's loyalty to him. It offered culturally conservative downstairs workers no real economic solutions—in fact his "America First" policies on tariffs and trade would hurt the majority of white workers and farmers—but pin-pointed economic problems that are incredibly important. We do need a transformation of the neo-liberal reigning US-sponsored corporate trade regime. By integrating issues of economic populism into the culture wars, Trump gave his base much stronger reason to back him, and called out aspects of the "globalist" or "cosmopolitan" liberal Blue elites that made both their economic policies and cultural arguments more problematic, weakening their ability to counter Trump's Security story and to defeat him politically.

Everyone as Enemy: The War of All Against All

Recall that Joe the Plumber, who we discussed at the beginning of Chapter 2, captured the zeitgeist of the Security story when he said:

> the more people who have guns the safer they will be.[43]

Asked about how many guns he has, he exclaims:

> not enough![44]

In 2014, Joe wrote an open letter to a father who lost his kid to a mass shooting:

> I am sorry you lost your child. I myself have a son and daughter and the one thing I never want to go through, is what you are going through now. But: As harsh as this sounds—your dead kids don't trump my Constitutional rights.[45]

Joe is signaling something important about the American Security story—and the direction recent presidents, especially Trump—have taken it. Joe is telling us that everybody needs a gun because everybody you meet is potentially an enemy. We need an armed America, as Trump has often said, because nobody is safe on the streets, in a restaurant, a workplace, a school or even one's own home.

The arming of America vastly multiplies the enemies in the Security story. The enemy of the true American is not just foreigners or the domestic fifth column of immigrants, Blacks and Muslims. The Security story now tells us that even members of our own tribe are a threat. This idea of everyone-as-enemy is an expansive Security story that finds fertile soil in capitalist societies and particularly in the militarized, cowboy capitalism of the US.[46]

This version of the Security story creates *a generalized fear of the other*, requiring security systems in your home, a gun on your person and a president tough enough to take control and impose a law-and-order regime at home. It means a militarization of the police, the schools and the home, where everybody has a gun and is trained to use it to fight off the enemy who is everyman.[47]

The Security story of everyone-as-enemy resonates in the capitalist house for several reasons. First, capitalism turns everyone into a competitor with everyone else. Competitors are rivals and the Security story blurs the line between being rivals in the market and outright enemies.

We see this with our students, who have to compete for good jobs in a highly competitive market.

> The competition begins early in life and breeds, they tell us, a generalized distrust and hostility of every other student in college, even students of the same race, religion or gender as they are. Students know they have to get higher grades than their classmates and report that the competition colors all their interactions with all other students, even those who are their friends. It doesn't mean they hate each other, but it puts them on guard, always holding back and being careful not to disclose subject material in study groups that might lead others to do better than they do.[48]

This competitive self-centeredness produces a student culture of subtle fear. The competition for grades and jobs can turn students into rivals or enemies not just in the classroom but in parties, dating and drinking binges.

As with students, capitalism turns all workers into competitors with all other workers, who can become bitter rivals and enemies as well. Again, this is a competition that doesn't just inflame fear across racial or ethnic lines but turns white workers against other white workers and Blacks against Blacks.

> On a June 9 National Public Radio news report, the local leader of a United Steel Workers Union in Granite City Illinois city steel planet told the NPR reporter that Trump's recent imposition of a 25% tariff on steel has made his fellow steel workers "jubilant." 800 steel jobs were coming back to his plant and workers felt their way of life might be saved. The reporter asked how these workers felt about their fellow American workers in "downstream" industries that had to buy more expensive steel for their products and might lose their own jobs because of the cost increase. The white local steel union leader showed no sympathy for 12,000 workers in other industries—hurt by the steel tariff. He said that they had been making money off cheap steel dumped from other countries, and it was about time that they paid the price.[49]

A Security story that turns not only Black worker against white worker but white workers against each other is doing its appointed job heroically. The whole purpose of the Security story is to keep the down-stairs workers from uniting with each other against their upstairs corporate bosses. The everyone-as-enemy story not only pits every downstairs worker against each other, but prompts them to look upstairs to help them win the downstairs competition. The downstairs steel workers congratulated the upstairs steel company CEOs and Trump for securing tariffs that allow them to get jobs and better wages at the expense of other workers who would lose jobs and be stuck with lower wages.

Beyond fueling antagonistic competition of all against all, capitalism also makes money off of generalized fear of the other. Consider just two examples: the home security companies and the gun manufacturers. It's impossible not to notice the explosion in the marketing of home security systems when you're watching cable news. There is the omni-present ad of women sitting and talking in their living room when some

menacing looking guys approach their house looking to get in and rob
them. With a smile, the women inside turn to their computer monitor
and activate a visual alarm and lighting system that scares the daylights
out of the intruders, who turn around and flee. A sign of the home security company planted in the front lawn reminds the viewer it's time to
keep your family safe by *buying the security system*, which allows you on
your cell phone even when you're away from home to see if somebody
is approaching your house. You can police the local enemy and protect
your home and family wherever you are.

The organization leading the crusade for the everyone-as-enemy
Security story is the National Rifle Association (NRA), a trade association of gun manufacturers who make a fortune off selling weapons to as
many Americans as possible. Close to President Trump and most earlier
presidents, the NRA has had a stranglehold on politicians, laws and
popular feelings about the need for everyone to have guns. Its executive
director, Wayne LaPierre, is famous for his slogan:

> The only thing that stops a bad guy with a gun is a good guy with
> a gun.[50]

This has led Trump and other presidents as well as a vast majority
of Republicans and many Democrats in Congress to champion arming
teachers as the best way to stop mass school shooters. Putting more
guns in the schools by arming both teachers and students is the core of
the Security story pact when it comes to protecting school kids, like the
ones who rose up against such insanity, after a fellow student shot 19
of their own at the Parkland school 2018 massacre in Florida. Wayne
LaPierre said after an earlier school shooting:

> I call on Congress today to act immediately to appropriate what-
> ever is necessary to put armed officers in every single school in this
> nation.[51]

The NRA maximizes profits by helping enshrine a Security story
of everyone-as-enemy. If everyone endangers you, then everyone needs
a gun to feel safe. There are already about 350 million guns owned by

Americans, more than the entire US population, since many house-holds stock huge arsenals. Gun companies know that only about a third of Americans own guns, and if they can get the other two-thirds to embrace the everyone-as-enemy story, they will make a fortune.

One new profitable market might be guns for women after the expo-sure of so much sexual harassment and violence against women in the #MeToo movement. In the workplace and even at home, the story of everyone-as-enemy can apply even to intimates, including married cou-ples. When distrust is rampant in the culture, it filters into the family and can lead spouses to see each other as possible enemies. The #MeToo movement has opened up a new market for guns in families where we know domestic violence is all too common, including husbands against wives, wives against husbands, children against parents and parents against children. The family in the evolving Security story is less a haven in the heartless world but another world of insecurity, bullying and vio-lence, where gun companies can find a new profitable market to make money, including selling chic pink guns women can tuck away in their purses. A huge set of websites advertise guns for women, with the fol-lowing sales pitch marketing to women:

> What guns are women buying? Well, we know that each woman can only know which is the right one for her, but here are the top 10 choices women are making when purchasing a handgun which can help to narrow the field of options for you. Remember, what is right for one woman may not be right for another, so when making your choice it is important to consider all of the variables that may be unique to you such as, hand size, recoil sensitivity, location and reach of the controls and their ease of operation. Get to a gun store and get your hands on numerous models and if possible, rent or try these models on the range. Trust me, you will know the right one when you find it.

> I find a number of things very interesting in this list. One, women are primarily buying semi-automatic handguns with a slight majority of them choosing a 9mm. The other fascinating thing is that 3 of the top 10 guns women are choosing are Glocks, which

historically has not been known as a woman's favorite brand. These clear preferences help put to rest such myths as; a woman needs a smaller caliber, she should have a revolver or she should have . . . fill in the blank. You can see by the variety below, that there is NO ONE RIGHT GUN for a woman or any one feature that makes a gun a "woman's gun". Now, I am not nixing revolvers, as both number eleven and twelve came in as revolvers. Many women prefer them and they are the better choice if one's primary mode of carry is in a concealed carry purse. But clearly, women are breaking some of the stereotypes usually placed on them.[52]

Two other elements of US capitalism help the population resonate with the everyone-as-enemy chapter of the Security story. One is the obvious fact that American capitalists have embraced militarism as a way to ensure global profits and access to markets everywhere on the planet. A militarized society indoctrinates the population with the moral necessity of fighting and defeating the enemy, wherever he or she may be. Since all US soldiers are called "heroes" for fighting, ordinary Americans are learning from the evolving Security story that they too can be heroes in the war at home. It is their moral responsibility to arm themselves to protect themselves and their families. Since Americans have learned to view the world as a Hobbesian jungle of enemies, upstairs elites can more easily transfer that view to life on the home front. An armed America—for war abroad and against the Hobbesian enemies in your own neighborhood—is the only America that the Security story proclaims is safe. And a bully nation abroad creates a bully culture at home, all in the name of strength and protection.[53]

US capitalism also offers fertile soil for the everyone-as-enemy story by its atomized and individualistic culture. In the US capitalist model, in contrast to the European alternative, it's "sink or swim" on your own. Everyone is responsible for himself or herself and, as the famed capitalist champion, Ayn Rand, put it, the greatest immorality is to look out for others at the expense of oneself. One of Rand's books is called *The Virtue of Selfishness*, and it promotes the ultimate morality of each individual looking out for himself or herself:

The man who does not value himself, cannot value anything or anyone. . . . An Individualist is a man who lives for his own sake and by his own mind; he neither sacrifices himself to others nor sacrifices others to himself; he deals with men as a trader.[54]

The American Dream tells us that the US is exceptional because it gives everyone the opportunity to organize their life based on Rand's concept of the moral "virtue of selfishness." This "me, me, me" notion of the American Dream is an extension of the competition in all capitalist societies, explicitly affirming the moral value of self-interest. It fuels a form of competitiveness that breeds intensified distrust of everyone else, since it becomes morally suspect for any person to give up his or her egoistic pursuits to help others. This is a moral recipe to regard everyone as a potential enemy, if only by making clear that indifference to their needs is less important than gratifying one's own.[55]

Every capitalist Security story is, in the end, about how to prevent those downstairs from creating the solidarity that can challenge the upstairs. Individualism is a formidable barrier to that solidarity, since everyone downstairs is eyeing each other with distrust and a sense of responsibility only to oneself. The sociologist Emile Durkheim argued that such atomization is a suicide pact, since it creates isolation and loneliness leading many to suicidal depression. But it also allows Americans to chase their own star and live out the self-centered life the American Dream promises, while counting on the upstairs rulers to hold the house together and give everyone a minimal sense of connection to their rulers.

What might be called atomization-by-design is integral to American capitalism—and, in some degree, to all capitalist societies. Solidarity is the enemy of capitalism, and its Security story is crafted to ensure that the downstairs will be fighting each other rather than joining to fight the 1% upstairs. The everyone-is-enemy chapter of that story may, in the end, be its most important narrative, because there is no more powerful barrier to war between upstairs and downstairs than war among everyone downstairs. Nor is there any greater incentive for the downstairs to seek solidarity with the upstairs.

The everyone-as-enemy story has one other supremely important virtue for the capitalist upstairs. If everyone downstairs fears and distrusts everyone else as an enemy, inevitably the population will be frightened to the point that they seek an ever more powerful ruler upstairs. A Hobbesian war downstairs is a marvelous recipe for an authoritarian house that vests power upstairs to police the war and ensure protection. The more chaotic and fearful the downstairs people feel, the more they are likely to beg the upstairs to take all the necessary power to control the house and ensure order. This is, of course, a recipe for capitalism authoritarianism and a path toward neo-fascism, the subject of our next chapter.

4

FROM CAPITALISM TO FASCISM

THE SECURITY STORY AND
THE FALL OF DEMOCRACY

I'm afraid based on my own experience that fascism will come to America in the name of national security.

—Jim Garrison

Benito Mussolini created the word "fascism." He defined it as "the merging of the state and the corporation." He also said a more accurate word would be "corporatism." This was the definition in Webster's up until 1987 when a corporation bought Webster's and changed it to exclude any mention of corporations.

—Adam McKay

The American fascists are most easily recognized by their deliberate perversion of truth and fact. Their newspapers and propaganda carefully cultivate every fissure of disunity, every crack in the common front against fascism.

—Henry A. Wallace

I wonder if you are ashamed of calling a Democratically elected government a fascist government.

—Medea Benjamin

In June 2018, the world learned that the freedom of the American press was under serious attack. The Justice Department told Ali Watkins, a

New York Times reporter, that it had been secretly taking her private emails and phone records for several years, as part of an investigation into leaks. The story rocked the country:

> The *New York Times* revealed on June 7 that the Justice Department had seized records for two email accounts and a mobile account belonging to *Times* reporter Ali Watkins in connection with an investigation into alleged leaks of information regarding the Senate Select Committee on Intelligence (SSCI) probe into Russian interference in the 2017 presidential election. The data, from Watkins' Verizon and Google accounts spanned years. Watkins was informed of the seizure in a letter from the Justice Department.[1]

The *New York Times* had not been informed earlier nor had Watkins. Millions of Americans woke up to a new stage of US history. Might this be the beginning of Big Brother in America? Here was a president attacking the press as an enemy of national security. Warnings from media groups were ominous, summarized in a *New York Times* story:

> The Committee to Protect Journalists called the move "a fundamental threat to press freedom." The Times, in its own statement, called the seizure "an outrageous overreach" and raised concerns about a chilling effect on journalists' ability to report on the government.[2]

President Trump had worked hard to demonize the press by constantly tweeting that it was "fake news." The Justice Department's attack on the reporter went further, the kind of physical intimidation of media that is one of the hallmarks of fascism.

Moreover, Trump had already called freedom of the press "disgusting," and attacked it savagely, as documented by the American Civil Liberties Union (ACLU):

> Trump the candidate also blacklisted reporters and entire news outlets from campaign events, referred to journalists as "scum"

and "slime," and mocked a reporter for having a disability . . . he threatened a lawsuit against a Hispanic journalist group for calling out his bigoted remarks.

"I would never kill them but I do hate them," he said of reporters. "And some of them are such lying, disgusting people."[3]

Trump's Security story—like that of Nazi Germany—highlighted the press as one of the great enemies of the nation. On June 12, 2018, Trump called the free press—naming CNN and NBC—as "enemies of the people" and then "the country's main enemies."[4] This followed Trump's many racist policies and authoritarian rhetoric detailed in the last chapter, his effusive praise and affection for dictators and strongmen ruling nations from Saudi Arabia to North Korea to Russia, his embrace of his advisor's Steve Bannon white nationalism, calling out as "fine people" some of the neo-Nazi groups marching in Charlottesville, Virginia, and his backing of Republican candidates identified with neo-Nazi and Confederate white supremacist groups, his call to lock up thousands of kids in military facilities or internment camps and deport immigrants without constitutionally mandated judicial review of asylum seekers, all reminiscent of the explicitly authoritarian and racist policies at the center of Hitler's Germany.

Not surprisingly, Trump has spurred the rise of a cottage industry of books warning that fascism, which wiped out the free press, has become a real possibility. Former Secretary of State, Madeline Albright, hardly an alarmist or apocalyptic figure, wrote a 2018 book called *Fascism: A Warning*,[5] seeing a perilous spread of neo-fascist parties and governments in Europe and in the US. Steven Levitsky and Daniel Ziblatt penned another best-seller called *How Democracies Die*.[6] And sober, influential academics, such as Yale political scientist, Timothy Snyder, wrote his 2017 best-seller book, *On Tyranny*,[7] and his 2018 book, *The Road to Unfreedom*,[8] to explain German fascism in the 20th century and the chilling path that both Europe and the US could take to resurrect that nightmare.

Trump played an important role, because his Security story and tweets were so nakedly bigoted and authoritarian. But the capitalist house has always flirted with the dark elements of the Security story, prompting a long history of concern about fascism coming to America. In the 1980s, Bertram Gross wrote *Friendly Fascism*[9] about a soft American fascism emerging under President Reagan. In 2004, in the era of George W. Bush, the novelist Philip Roth wrote about the coming of fascism in America in his dystopian novel, *The Plot Against America*.[10] As far back as 1936, novelist Sinclair Lewis wrote the famous book, *It Can't Happen Here*.[11] These books were written long before Trump became president, suggesting that the US system has long been perceived as one that could morph into authoritarianism or neo-fascism.

The new explosion of books is a response to Trump's version of the Security story that cultivates rage, fear and surrender to "strongmen" leaders such as Trump himself, who are elected or legally appointed but, like Hitler, are poised to destroy democracy. Snyder, an expert on German fascism, writes:

> The mistake is to assume that rulers who came to power through institutions cannot change or destroy those very institutions—even when that is exactly what they have announced that they will do.[12]

Snyder notes importantly that real crises that threaten the economic security and cultural respect of the downstairs give license to the authoritarian stories of such leaders:

> Both fascism and communism were responses to globalization: to the real and perceived inequalities it created, and the apparent helplessness of the democracies in addressing them. Fascists rejected reason in the name of will, denying objective truth in favor of a glorious myth articulated by leaders who claimed to give voice to the people.

> Democracy failed in Europe in the 1920s, '30s, and '40s, and it is failing not only in much of Europe but in many parts of the world today. It is that history and experience that reveals to us the dark range of our possible futures. A nationalist will say that "it can't happen here," which is the first step toward disaster.[13]

It is the reality of the downstairs real grievances and understand-
able fears that opens the door wide to the strongmen and makes their
Security story emotionally attractive and resonant. Trump and earlier
presidents have had success with the Security story because the downstairs lack voice and are losing economic and psychological security. But
the Security stories that Trump (and also Reagan and Bush offered) are
not offering solutions to these very real downstairs crises. In fact, their
policies and cultural stories make the downstairs more vulnerable.

The Security story "works" in all these cases, though because much,
though not all, of the despairing downstairs is ready for it, triggered by
economic and cultural fears more than reasoned hope. The system is
not working, in fact, for millions of working people downstairs. Trump's
story breaks the guard rails of democracy in the name of protecting
these "forgotten people"—against countries engaging in unfair trade,
against terrorist foreigners and illegal immigrants, and against internal
tribal enemies or imposters who threaten traditional family values. With
mainstream parties not solving real grievances, the authoritarian leader
becomes an attractive alternative as he promises to make the nation
great again, using powers unchecked by Congress and corrupt politicians. Writing of Hitler and almost certainly thinking about Trump,
Snyder writes:

> People who assure you that you can only gain security at the price
> of liberty usually want to deny you both.[14]

Hitler enacted the darkest side of the Security story, using it to turn
a highly civilized and democratic nation to genocide and dictatorship.
*Throughout history, the Security story has been the narrative that leaders have
used to take societies to barbarism. Nazi Germany proved that it remains the
most dangerous story ever told*, and we show in this chapter how Hitler
crafted the Nazi version of the narrative and why so many millions of
Germans embraced it.

The chilling reality is that the economic, political and cultural conditions that allowed Hitler to be elected are resurfacing, both reflecting and fueling the current relevance and strength of his Security story.

A remarkable Netflix film, an absolute must-see, called *Look Who's Back*, is a story of how a reincarnated Hitler returns today to Germany and takes back power. Looking exactly like Hitler, with all his fascist ideas and salutes, but rising to fame today in the persona of a media celebrity, he finds a remarkably receptive audience to his Security story. The 2017 success of the new neo-fascist party in Germany, the Alternative for Germany (AFD), winning the third most seats in 2017 in the Reichstag, shows this is anything but cinematic fantasy.

Any American watching *Look Who's Back* will immediately think about Trump. But while Europe was more vulnerable to fascism than the US, the threat of some form of fascism could play out in America. The president plays a crucial role, but it is the underlying culture and political economy that sends chills down the spine. For it is the rising inequality and economic insecurity, inflamed by bitter culture wars dividing the nation, both in Germany and the US, that causes leaders to turn to the Security story. And it is the fertile soil within a fevered and mobilized minority of the German (and now perhaps of the American) population that allows the story and storytellers to turn capitalist democracy into an authoritarian, even fascist, system.

The Security story builds on inbred features of capitalism disposing it to authoritarian rule. Our long complacency about the impossibility of losing democracy is over. In fact, we can now see that there are many features of capitalism and its Security story that create a persistent risk of our morphing into a form of "capitalist fascism." These include:

- *The deep inequalities and injustices of the upstairs/downstairs capitalist house*
- *The enormous power that inbred inequality vests in the capitalist upstairs elites*
- *The receptivity of major sections of the downstairs working classes to authoritarian rule*
- *The periodic economic and social crises that put the house at risk and elicit hunger for a strongman to keep it together*
- *The capitalist elites' willingness to create endless enemies to consolidate power, even if it means turning to authoritarian rule.*

In the light of all this, our complacency about the strength of our democracy needs to be replaced by a deep concern about the authoritarian dimensions that are inbred in American capitalism and the commitment to a struggle to prevent the house from morphing into fascism based on the power of the most dangerous story ever told. Elites are constantly tempted and clearly willing to use it, whatever the cost to democracy.

How Germany Went Fascist: Hitler's Security Story

European fascism began in Italy, when Benito Mussolini created his fascist party 10 years before Hitler took power in Germany. Mussolini had been a socialist before World War I but he came to believe that class struggle—of the downstairs workers against the capitalist upstairs—was doomed. He felt that socialists had failed to understand that "class interests" were too narrow to mobilize working people, who are more powerfully moved by "psychological and moral considerations that transcend them." Economics and class solidarity could never be the basis of community for workers and would destroy the nation.[15]

Instead, Mussolini said, the nation itself is the unifying force, creating a spiritual bond more powerful than just economic interests. "Class," he wrote:

> is based on the community of interests but the nation is a history of sentiments of tradition of language of culture of race.[16]

Later, he elaborated that:

> The fatherland is the hard and solid ground, the millarian product of the race . . . the community of blood . . . to conduct the struggle against nature, misery, ignorance, impotence and slavery of every form in which men find themselves in the state of nature.[17]

He also argued that the state is a moral hierarchy led by a single all-powerful figure and a fascist party who can unify and protect against all enemies the people in a true "community of blood." This points to the legitimating story of fascism as a society unified by "blood" (essentially meaning race) and "spiritual renaissance" shared by the true members of the tribe, whether rich or poor, living upstairs or downstairs. The downstairs will renounce class warfare—partly because Mussolini promised policies that would help create jobs and economic growth—and eagerly join with the nation's leaders upstairs because they are, thereby, realizing the destiny built into their deepest spiritual nature. They are joining their community of blood. Fascist leaders in the upstairs—exercising absolute authority—will protect all members of the house or nation from the decay and injustice caused by the nation's enemies, while restoring the honor and status of the true tribal members in the world's greatest nation.

Hitler created a genocidal form of fascism called Nazism, but we will call it fascist since almost all political scientists see it as such. Hitler embraced a variant of Mussolini's Security story in *Mein Kampf*,[18] his manifesto which became a best-seller second only to the Bible. In this white-hot hyper-nationalist polemic, Hitler spelled out his own argument about how as the Führer or Great Leader, he could protect all true members of the German nation—whether living upstairs or downstairs in the house. As dictator of a globally dominant German Third Reich, he would unite the Aryan race—the blood community of authentic Germans—who together formed the only genuinely creative and spiritual nation in the world, indeed the nation most highly blessed by God.

> Our enemies must not deceive themselves—in the 2,000 years of German history known to us, our people have never been more united than today. The Lord of the Universe has treated us so well in the past years that we bow in gratitude to a providence which has allowed us to be members of such a great nation.[19]

Hitler's Security story is that he—the omnipotent leader of the nation—will command a holy Aryan war to destroy all the enemies who were threatening the survival of sacred Germany. Like Mussolini, Hitler rejected the idea that class struggle between the upstairs capitalist elites and downstairs workers would or should distract workers, since humans are deeply moved only by higher moral purposes embodied in

the Aryan nation. Material interests need to be met but they are narrow and divisive. Only the spiritual greatness of the German nation
could unify all true Germans, offering them protection from mortal
enemies and giving their life meaning and the full respect and honor
they deserve. The nation is an organic spiritual force far more important
than narrow economic interests, as Hitler makes clear in *Mein Kampf*:

> The State is a community of living beings who have kindred phys-
> ical and spiritual natures, organized for the purpose of assuring
> the conservation of their own kind and to help towards fulfilling
> those ends which Providence has assigned to that particular race
> or racial branch. Economic activity is one of the many auxiliary
> means which are necessary for the attainment of those aims. But
> economic activity is never the origin or purpose of a State, except
> where a State has been originally founded on a false and unnatural
> basis.[20]

Hitler's nationalism unifies and protects all pure Germans, with
Aryan racial solidarity preventing class warfare between the German
upstairs and downstairs:

> A State has never arisen from commercial causes for the purpose
> of peacefully serving commercial ends; but States have always
> arisen from the instinct to maintain the racial group, . . . But as
> soon as economic interests begin to predominate over the racial
> and cultural instincts in a people or a State, these economic inter-
> ests unloose the causes that lead to subjugation and oppression.[21]

Nation trumps class, since material interests can only divide the
nation's upstairs and downstairs—and lead to corrupt tyranny. Hitler offered robust economic protection to German workers, and his
nationalistic agenda, like Trump's, offers jobs and economic security
to a Germany in economic crisis. Fighting the enemies meant spending enormous sums on military investments that would stimulate
growth and create millions of jobs. So while fascism subordinates economic interests to spiritual fulfillment and racial purity, it promises the

downstairs workers massive economic gains as it leads the fight against Germany's enemies.

But Hitler makes clear that any downstairs worker movement led by decadent and class-driven socialists or Jews (the racial enemy of the nation at the time) would destroy the sacred unity of the nation. Here's Hitler on how Left parties, specifically the ruling Social Democrats, poison the nation when they advocate socialism:

> Everything was disparaged—the nation, because it was held to be an invention of the "capitalist" class (how often I had to listen to that phrase!); the Fatherland, because it was held to be an instrument in the hands of the bourgeoisie for the exploitation of the working masses; the authority of the law, because that was a means of holding down the proletariat; religion, as a means of doping the people, so as to exploit them afterwards; morality, as a badge of stupid and sheepish docility. There was nothing that they did not drag in the mud.
>
> . . . During those days of mental anguish and deep meditation I saw before my mind the ever-increasing and menacing army of people who could no longer be reckoned as belonging to their own nation.[22]

Fascism is white Aryan nationalism in the German case. Hitler's legitimating story of fascism embraces capitalist companies and private investment to create a mighty militarized economy, but it is not built on capitalist rationality—or, indeed, any kind of rationality. Its aim is furthering God's aim to protect the sacred German nation of the Aryan race—the true community of blood.

Hitler's fascist Security story is to protect Germans from foreign enemies and from the domestic Jewish, socialist imposters who could never be members of the blood community of the Aryan nation. Before invading Poland and starting World War II, Hitler often talked about his desire for and love of peace, but he let slip his true intent—his war would be merciless:

I want war. To me all means will be right. My motto is not "Don't, whatever you do, annoy the enemy." My motto is "Destroy him by all and any means." I am the one who will wage the war![23]

By destroying the racially poisonous Jews and secular urban Leftists who were populating the decadent German cities, and by defeating the foreign enemies who had humiliated Germany, he would reconstruct the community of "blood and soil" that would "make Germany great again." His rebuilding of the nation would create an economic power-house securing jobs for the workers. But the essence of Hitler's Security story is rebuilding the economy as part of a much broader renewal of the exceptionalist Aryan nation, a kind of racialized hyper-nationalism that would give the "true" Germans—those in the Aryan Nazi tribe—the recognition and respect they deserve so deeply. The parallels to American white nationalism in the Trumpian Security story are striking—and hard to ignore.

Getting to Fascism: Hitler's Security Agenda in Four Steps

Hitler is very explicit in *Mein Kampf* about his fascist agenda:

> What we have to fight for is the necessary security for the existence and increase of our race and people, the subsistence of its children and the maintenance of our racial stock unmixed, the freedom and independence of the Fatherland; so that our people may be enabled to fulfil the mission assigned to it by the Creator.[24]

This agenda—achieving security and fulfillment of the great Fatherland—can only be won by *four great steps*, spelled out as follows, largely in Hitler's own words.

1. Put the Dear Leader in Power

Only a Great Leader—that is, an all-powerful, unchecked leader or Führer—can rally the people together in the service of uniting to save the nation. This requires moving away from democracy to embrace a dictator, the first great step toward fascism. Hitler is explicit that democracy runs against the "aristocratic" or authoritarian grain of nature:

> The parliamentary principle of vesting legislative power in the decision of the majority rejects the authority of the individual and puts a numerical quota of anonymous heads in its place. In doing so it contradicts the aristocratic principle, which is a fundamental law of nature.[25]

In other words, only an authoritarian nation is natural. Hitler argues that ordinary people understand this law of nature, and want to follow a strongman who alone can give them a sense of security:

> The PSYCHE of the broad masses is accessible only to what is strong and uncompromising. Like a woman whose inner sensibilities are not so much under the sway of abstract reasoning but are always subject to the influence of a vague emotional longing for the strength that completes her being, and who would rather bow to the strong man than dominate the weakling—in like manner the masses of the people prefer the ruler to the suppliant and are filled with a stronger sense of mental security by a teaching that brooks no rival than by a teaching which offers them a liberal choice.[26]

The rise of democracy, Hitler argues, simply reflects the cunning strategy of the inferior races, especially Jews, who are propagating a myth of social democracy or socialism benefiting only themselves and unfit for the German nation:

> The Right has further completely forgotten that democracy is fundamentally not German: it is Jewish. It has completely forgotten that this Jewish democracy with its majority decisions has always been without exception only a means towards the destruction of any existing Aryan leadership. . . . And that can be achieved by the man who can lie most artfully, most infamously; and in the last

resort he is not the German, he is, in Schopenhauer's words, "the great master in the art of lying"—the Jew.[27]

Democracy is not a German idea, nor an idea of any great nation. Foreign and internal enemies foisted it on Germany after its defeat in World War I. Jews, who Hitler argued were all socialists and led the Social Democratic liberal party, created the Weimar German Republic of the 1920s, which Hitler despised. Its Jewishness, secularism and socialism were a knife in the heart of the German nation.

Only a relentless strongman can mobilize the masses against this unnatural system which bred insecurity by weakening the Aryan nation and pitting the German downstairs majority against its upstairs elites. It is important to note that Hitler did not see fascism as anti-capitalist; his Nazi program could be seen as a regime change from capitalist democracy to capitalist fascism. Hitler believed that only a strongman like himself could unite the capitalist downstairs and upstairs in a fight to save the true German nation. Capitalism would survive but it would serve the Aryan nation rather than the reverse.

Hitler believed fervently in the politics of emotion that would turn an insecure people from democracy to dictatorship. He could appeal to an anxious populace ready to surrender everything for the great leader who alone can protect them and restore their greatness. Political scientist, Timothy Snyder, tells this story about Hitler:

> One of his former students implored him to "abandon yourself to your feelings, and you must always focus on the Führer's greatness, rather than on the discomfort you are feeling at present." Twelve years later, after all the atrocities, and at the end of a war that Germany had clearly lost, an amputated soldier told (Victor) Klemperer (a literary scholar of Jewish origins) that Hitler "has never lied yet. I believe in Hitler." The final mode is misplaced faith. It involves the sort of self-deifying claims the president made when he said that "I alone can solve it" or "I am your voice." When faith descends from heaven to earth in this way, no room remains for the small truths of our individual discernment and experience.

What terrified Klemperer was the way that this transition seemed permanent. Once truth had become oracular rather than factual, evidence was irrelevant.[28]

This illustrates one of the darkest sides of fascism and Hitler's Security story. It is based not just on extreme authority and emotionalism, but a cultivation and worship of the Irrational. Embedded in religion, mysticism and an exclusionary and violent devotion to the Tribe, Nation or Great Leader, this authoritarian version of the Security story became a legitimating force behind some of history's worst tyrannies, whether brutal Roman emperors like Caligula or Nazi leaders such as Hitler.

Hitler made no bones about the power of the irrational and his commitment to an emotional racialized politics that spoke to ordinary people's most primitive needs for security, survival and pride or respect. It is no surprise that Germans listening to Hitler's feverish nationalist passions—an explicit cultivation of the "irrational"—would themselves become passionate, as Hitler predicted:

> The doom of a nation can be averted only by a storm of flowing passion, but only those who are passionate themselves can arouse passion in others.[29]

Many supporters reported that embracing the Great Führer was like *"falling in love."* Material economic or class interests by themselves, Hitler argued, never can or should generate the emotions of fascist nationalism, which touch people's deepest spiritual needs and unify them to fight all enemies to save themselves, their sense of worth or honor, and their nation that creates and reflects their own spiritual greatness. Hitler made this explicit:

> Our clever "statesmen" were greatly amazed at this change of feeling. They never understood that as soon as man is called upon to struggle for purely material causes he will avoid death as best he can; for death and the enjoyment of the material fruits of a victory are quite incompatible concepts. The frailest woman will become a heroine when the life of her own child is at stake. And only the

will to save the race and native land or the State, which offers protection to the race, has in all ages been the urge which has forced
men to face the weapons of their enemies.[30]

Hitler's success in winning power helps demonstrate one of the
Right's great strengths: its explicit and powerful use of emotion, which
has often historically triumphed over the Left's appeal to rationality.
Hitler didn't entirely reject reason—a few could respond to it—but
relied on emotion to win the masses:

I use emotion for the many and reserve reason for the few.[31]

His Security story said that the emotional stress of insecurity ensured
the transition of a democratic majority to a mobilized fascist minority
desperate for an all-powerful Führer who would save them, their rightful honor and stature in society, and the nation itself.

It's worth noting that the shift toward authoritarian leadership is a
major shift from capitalist democracy, but it builds, as noted earlier, on
authoritarian tendencies within our present system. Capitalism is by
nature hierarchical, since it gives authority over the economy and the
workplace to owners of the firm, while workers must submit to corporate and managerial authority or risk being fired. Capitalism is an
authoritarian, not a democratic, economy.

Likewise, capitalist democracy politically favors the rich over the
poor and vests power with the capitalist elites. The capitalist upstairs—
whether Wall Street or politically engaged billionaires such as the Koch
Brothers or the Mercer family or Sheldon Adelson—dominate our politics and help shape the agendas of both Republicans and Democrats.

Capitalist democracy thus lays parts of the authoritarian floor on
which capitalist fascism can build. Trump shows most clearly how those
inbred authoritarian foundations can be politically leveraged by strongman presidents, who are capable of moving our system into a far more
authoritarian model. Hitler did not destroy corporations or the market
when he enshrined fascism, making clear why capitalists of his day ultimately preferred him to the Left. Fascism was profitable for capitalists,

hinting why they might entertain a shift toward capitalist authoritarianism. All this gives pause, because it offers institutional reasons why it might not be as difficult as many of us have assumed to move from capitalism to fascism.

2. Follow Nature's Law of Brute Strength Over Weakness

The second great step in the fascist agenda is a cultural revolution in which democratic weakness is transformed into authoritarian strength. The Great Leader would reflect and build this pillar of fascist culture. He would symbolize dominance and brute force—and would carry out a program, as prescribed by the fascist Security story—of violently destroying the nation's enemies, including democracy itself. There will be no mercy or compassion because the war for the nation can only be won and its people only made secure by a relentless cultivation of brute force. Sheer willpower of the Führer will build and perpetuate this culture of strength since the Great Leader acts in perpetuity to instruct the whole nation in the politics of extermination. Fascism's first and primary goal—the security of the nation—is to eliminate the inherently weak "parasites" who always threaten to sap the vitality and undermine the very survival of the nation.

Hitler sees domination of the weak by the strong as the primal law of nature:

> The stronger must dominate and not mate with the weaker, which would signify the sacrifice of its own higher nature. Only the born weakling can look upon this principle as cruel, and if he does so it is merely because he is of a feebler nature and narrower mind; for if such a law did not direct the process of evolution then the higher development of organic life would not be conceivable at all.[32]

Hitler makes clear that life is preparation for the never-ending fight for survival and the nation:

> Those who want to live, let them fight, and those who do not want to fight in this world of eternal struggle do not deserve to live.[33]

To live is to fight, and to fight is to embrace violence as the underpinning of all security and success:

> The very first essential for success is a perpetually constant and regular employment of violence.[34]

The culture of strength and force is, again, not a complete break from our current capitalist order. Capitalism is a culture of ruthless competition. As noted in Chapter 3, its Security story turns everyone into a rival and potential enemy of everyone else. To succeed, one must gird one's loins for struggle to move up the corporate ladder.

That struggle does not typically turn physically violent. But we live in a society of guns and violence, at home and abroad, that makes violence and brute force part of our heritage. Combined with perpetual fierce economic competition, such pervasive violence breeds an American psychology disposed toward power and despising weakness. Such continuities are yet another sign of why the shift from capitalist democracy to capitalist fascism might be easier than traditionally believed.

3. Destroy the Foreign Enemy

Hitler's third step to fascism involved mobilizing the German nation—both upstairs and downstairs together—to destroy its foreign enemies and ensure they could never defeat Germany again. Hitler claimed that he loved peace, but his Security story was built on the ashes of the humiliating defeat of Germany after World War I. The war not only killed millions of Germans, but also created a surrender so humiliating and economically devastating that it transformed the German view of the world and the need for overwhelming military power.

Hitler's Security story essentially said: Never Again! Fascism would never permit Germany to become weak and vulnerable to a repetition of disastrous defeat from foreign powers. Hitler saw his most important task as building a Third Reich so powerful that it would dominate Europe and perhaps the world, one that could crush any enemy.

At the end of the "Great War," the Allies—the US, Great Britain and France—determined that they would punish Germany with harsh penalties. The 1919 Versailles Treaty—that dictated the terms of German surrender and defeat—included economic reparations that created a German economic disaster, including hyper-inflation and mass unemployment. The great British economist, John Maynard Keynes, a prominent advisor during the peace talks, predicted the enormity of the disaster, leaving the negotiations in a state of fury and writing a famous book, *The Economic Consequences of the Peace*,[35] prophetically arguing that it ruined any prospect of future peace.

Hitler's militaristic agenda grew out of the Versailles Treaty, which obsessed him. He wrote and spoke endlessly about it, promising that the Nazi aim was to abolish the treaty and prevent any future humiliation of Germany:

> My program was to abolish the Treaty of Versailles. It is futile nonsense for the rest of the world to pretend today that I did not reveal this program until 1933, or 1935, or 1937. Instead of listening to the foolish chatter of émigrés, these gentlemen would have been wiser to read what I have written—and rewritten thousands of times. No human being has declared or recorded what he wanted more often than I. Again and again I wrote these words—the Abolition of the Treaty of Versailles. Not because it was a quixotic idea of my own, but because the Treaty of Versailles was the greatest injustice and the most infamous maltreatment of a great nation in recorded history and because it was impossible for our nation to continue to exist in the future unless Germany was free of this stranglehold.[36]

Hitler argued that the Versailles Treaty changed the world order forever. Henceforth, it would only be the military victor—the strongest nation—that could prosper while the vanquished could never do so. Referring to Versailles, he wrote that:

> This was the beginning of a new world order, that is, of the so-called victors and vanquished, a world order wherein the victors had all the rights and the vanquished none at all.[37]

Hitler's fascist agenda was to ensure that his German Third Reich would be the victor in this "new world order." This aim would shape his Security story and his political agenda from his founding of the Nazi party in the early 1920s to his taking power in 1933 and rearming Germany into what he believed would be the global victor in what became World War II. In a telegram to Franklin D. Roosevelt in 1938, Hitler makes clear that every step of his rule had been devoted to creating a new Reich—an Aryan glorious nation—that could conquer any foreign nation while integrating all Aryan people into a great unified all-powerful Germany:

> To preclude threats from the outside world, I have not only united the German Volk politically, I have rearmed it militarily. Further, I have sought to tear to shreds page upon page of this Treaty, whose 448 articles represent the most dastardly outrage ever committed against a people and man. I have restored those provinces to the Reich which were stolen from it in 1919. I have led home to the Reich millions of despondent Germans torn from us. I have restored the one-thousand-year old, historic unity of the German Lebensraum.[38]

Note that Hitler begins by saying that his entire agenda was "to preclude threats from the outside world." This is the foundation of his Security story. It resonated deeply in a German populace which had been destroyed economically, culturally and politically in World War I. Millions of Germans would follow any strong leader who promised to protect them from the possibility of another Versailles.

Hitler's militaristic Security story was hardly new. The idea that the nation could only be protected by becoming stronger than any potential enemy nation is built deeply into America's own concept of "national security." In the American "realist" view, the world order is Hobbesian, and requires control or policing by an "exceptionalist" nation that sees every other nation as a potential threat to its security, and thus must act to secure its own vital interests as well as order and peace in a free world. In American "neo-conservatism," the second major school of US foreign policy, only the nation of great moral virtue, blessed by God, can and must assume defeat of global evil and assume the role of international dominance that Hitler sought—in fact, Hitler's aspirations were less geographically expansive than the American hegemonic vision of itself today. All this is yet another indication of how an American fascist Security story could take root in the US since "precluding threats from the outside world" and building a world under our nation's great power, blessed by God and protected from all enemies, is already part of our national security religion.

4. Destroy the Enemy Within

Hitler's Security story targets those living in the nation but outside the Aryan tribe as the most dangerous enemies of the nation. The fourth great step to fascism is to purge these parasitic imposters who try to divide the German house and pit upstairs against downstairs—and Aryan against Aryan. The Security story says that the great German Fatherland can only be safe and fulfill its sacred mission from God if it exterminates the domestic enemy through racial purification and the elimination of socialists, ensuring the survival and flourishing of the nation's "community of blood."

In promising to destroy these enemies, Hitler was stoking what we would describe as the culture wars in the 1920s German Weimar Republic. The "blue" German states were the ethnically diverse urban, secular and Leftist German regions where Jews were concentrated; they tended to be educated, professional and live on the mezzanine of the German house or in the union-organized working classes downstairs. The "red" German states were the rural, religious, culturally conservative German areas of peasants, small business and religious leaders and churches, linked to the German aristocracy and its capitalist elites.

As in the US, the reigning Security story divided Germans by race, religion and cultural values rather than by economic position or class. Fascism's Security story told the mass of peasant and Aryan German workers downstairs in an era of a great German Depression that their enemies were not the Aryan German aristocracy or capitalist elites upstairs but the culturally subversive and economically elitist Jewish, urban, socialist and secular imposters, who represented everything alien to the Aryan Fatherland. Hitler's Security story united the Aryan upstairs and downstairs to crush the imposters who were not true members of the tribe. In so doing, it preserved the house and the honor of the true members of the German nation—despite the great economic problems of those in the downstairs who might have turned against the German wealthy classes. Instead, it uplifted their sense of worth and self-respect, by getting them to identify with the Aryan traditional aristocracy and capitalist elites who were responsible for their economic problems but shared their traditional culture and racial spiritual greatness.

In the fascist Security story, Jews are the parasitic race at the heart of the crisis, but Hitler identifies four internal enemies, all intertwined with the Jews and imposters in the tribe. Hitler's Security story rests ultimately on race, since the nation is simply a vessel for the security and flourishing of the Aryan race, the most creative in the world. Hitler's fascist vision is, as noted earlier, Aryan white nationalism. Inferior races have seeped into the German house, posturing as part of the Aryan race, but actually operating as evil "parasites" undermining the creativity and unity of the German nation and undermining the greatness of the true German tribe. The Nazi Security story says the imposters must be exterminated, since they are like termites eating away the foundation of any house, thereby dividing by "red" vs "blue" Germans rather than the upstairs vs the downstairs, and undermining the respect and greatness of the forgotten true German race.

Jews are the prime parasitic enemy:

> People who can sneak their way, like parasites, into the human body politic and make others work for them under various pretences can form a State without possessing any definite delimited territory. This is chiefly applicable to that parasitic nation which, particularly at the present time preys upon the honest portion of mankind; I mean the Jews.

> The Jewish State has never been delimited in space. It has been spread all over the world, without any frontiers whatsoever, and

has always been constituted from the membership of one race exclusively. That is why the Jews have always formed a State within the State. One of the most ingenious tricks ever devised has been that of sailing the Jewish ship-of-state under the flag of Religion and thus securing that tolerance which Aryans are always ready to grant to different religious faiths.[39]

Hitler argues that Jews are the race with the cunning talent of melding into other nations, disguising their alien being and subverting the purity and unity of the Fatherland:

> He can live among other nations and States only as long as he succeeds in persuading them that the Jews are not a distinct people but the representatives of a religious faith who thus constitute a 'religious community', though this be of a peculiar character. . . . He is obliged to conceal his own particular character and mode of life that he may be allowed to continue his existence as a parasite among the nations. The greater the intelligence of the individual Jew, the better will he succeed in deceiving others. His success in this line may even go so far that the people who grant him hospitality may be led to believe that the Jew among them is a genuine Frenchman, for instance, or Englishman or German or Italian, who just happens to belong to a religious denomination which is different from that prevailing in these countries.[40]

Jews are the umbrella enemy in Hitler's Security story, because they lead all those outside the true German tribe: the intellectual secular urban classes, the socialist workers and immigrants. Jews have infused all these groups with anti-nationalistic values. They lack the ruthless toughness, the militarism, the rootedness in the land, the religious fervor, the authoritarian passion and the Aryan pride and nationalism that unite the German house. And they are responsible for the economic crisis and the cultural erosion that is undermining the Aryan downstairs and destroying the pride of the true German tribe, both upstairs and downstairs.

The Jews are leaders, argues Hitler, of the socialist parties and the trade unions, a second domestic enemy, who threaten the nation by dividing upstairs elites from downstairs workers. Hitler expresses sympathy with workers but makes clear that he sees their organized protests as a deep threat to the nation:

> I was able to understand their [fellow workers] position fully. They were dissatisfied with their lot and cursed the fate which had hit them so hard. They hated their employers, whom they looked upon as the heartless administrators of their cruel destiny. Often they used abusive language against the public officials, whom they accused of having no sympathy with the situation of the working people. They made public protests against the cost of living and paraded through the streets in defence of their claims. At least all this could be explained on reasonable grounds. But what was impossible to understand was the boundless hatred they expressed against their own fellow citizens, how they disparaged their own nation, mocked at its greatness, reviled its history and dragged the names of its most illustrious men in the gutter.
>
> This hostility towards their own kith and kin, their own native land and home was as irrational as it was incomprehensible. It was against Nature.[41]

As shown earlier, Hitler rages all the time against the Leftist and Jewish Social Democratic and Communist parties, a third domestic enemy, who are leading class warfare that divides the nation and represents a "war against Nature." They are turning German workers against their race and nation, which Hitler calls "incomprehensible." The economic well-being his Security story brings these workers comes from building the great Aryan nation, which will not only provide the best jobs for the workers as the country industrializes and militarizes but also give them the cultural respect and spiritual greatness that materialistic soulless parties and causes can never provide them.

The socialist worker movements and parties were being guided by a third enemy, the "intellectual class." Mainly urban, liberal and Jewish,

Hitler argues they are responsible for tearing down the cultural strength of the "Volk," the term used frequently by Hitler to describe the salt-of-the-earth Germans, connected to the land rather than the city and the true spiritual carriers of the Aryan race's common sense and fierce "willpower:"

> Our intellectual class, particularly in Germany, is so shut up in itself and fossilized that it lacks living contact with the classes beneath it. Two evil consequences result from this: First, the intellectual class neither understands nor sympathizes with the broad masses. It has been so long cut off from all connection with them that it cannot now have the necessary psychological ties that would enable it to understand them. It has become estranged from the people. Secondly, the intellectual class lacks the necessary willpower; for this faculty is always weaker in cultivated circles, which live in seclusion, than among the primitive masses of the people.[42]

Hitler argues, with some truth, that the intellectual classes are largely divorced from rural farmers, small town business people and ordinary religious people with traditional family values. They have no respect for the hardworking masses and have no understanding of their needs or psychology. Most of all, they lack the understanding of the masses' need for authoritarian Great Leaders who provide the brute strength and willpower that offers security and cultural self-respect for the masses.

The fourth domestic enemy will sound familiar today: the immigrants who are polluting the nation. Immigrants are all part of alien races, who can never be part of the community of blood. Hitler ridicules the ease with which immigrants are brought into Germany and turned into citizens in the German nation, an absurdity if they are not Aryans. Hitler mocks the immigration procedures:

> The whole process of acquiring civic rights is not very different from that of being admitted to membership of an automobile club, for instance. A person files his application. It is examined. It is sanctioned. And one day the man receives a card which informs him that he has become a citizen. The information is given in an

amusing way. An applicant who has hitherto been a Zulu or Kaffir is told: "By these presents you are now become a German Citizen."

The President of the State can perform this piece of magic. What God Himself could not do is achieved by . . . of a civil servant through a mere twirl of the hand. Nothing but a stroke of the pen, and a Mongolian slave is forthwith turned into a real German. Not only is no question asked regarding the race to which the new citizen belongs; even the matter of his physical health is not inquired into. His flesh may be corrupted with syphilis; but he will still be welcome in the State as it exists to-day so long as he may not become a financial burden or a political danger.[43]

Hitler's Security story requires a war against immigration, and he mocks immigrants here without reserve. How can a Zulu or Mongolian become a German—this is insane! The nation is nothing but the vehicle by which the Aryan race can fulfill its God-given creativity. Immigrants can never play a constructive role in building the Aryan race and nation that is the ultimate goal of fascism.

The fascist war against the four domestic enemies—prescribed by Hitler's Security story—is ultimately healthy for the nation. It unites the true members of the tribe—upstairs and downstairs—against the weakness of all these alien tribes. As Aryan peasants and workers, the true German Volk, unite with Aryan elites to defend their race and nation, they triumph in the culture wars that were beginning to tear Germany apart. Following their Führer, the German peasant and worker will regain their economic well-being while, even more import-ant, regaining their cultural dignity and self-respect which the tribal imposters have been arrogantly attacking as uneducated foolishness. Hitler's Security story restores jobs and spiritual fulfillment to the Ger-man "forgotten people."

Losing Democracy?: Four Steps Toward American Fascism

Many Americans are now worried that the four steps that took Germany from a great civilized democracy to fascism may already be underway in the US. President Trump is seen as the catalyst of this transformation, and he is indeed taking the nation toward an authoritarian capitalist model. Hitler's Security story and his four steps have many parallels to Trump's own agenda. Trumpism could become a recipe for American neo-fascism.

But the dangers are systemic—and go beyond Trump. Tendencies toward more concentration of power in the presidency and a focus on destroying both foreign and domestic enemies have been part of the Security story of almost all recent presidents. They have gone into high gear since the Reagan revolution and we conclude this chapter by briefly reviewing the four steps just described in Germany that are resurfacing in new ways here—and that could weaken or even end American democracy.

Put the Dear Leader in Power

At this writing, Trump has successfully created a cult of personality that allows him to act like a strongman ruler, not subject to the rule of law. During the Mueller special investigation of Russian meddling in the 2016 election, Trump claimed, as noted in Chapter 3, that he had the absolute right to pardon himself and repeated Nixon's words that when the president does it, it is not illegal. In other words, the president is above the law, one definition of a dictator. This move to institutionalize a shift from president to a "strongman" leader freed from constitutional checks and balances, is the first great step toward fascism.

At the 2016 Republican National Convention, Trump showed his authoritarian cards, saying only he could solve the nation's problems. This had all the echoes of a Dear Leader. Trump was saying that he alone was a savior who could be trusted with the unchecked power to secure the nation from all its enemies. Republicans at the convention erupted in approval:

> But when Trump said, "I am your voice," the delegates on the con-
> vention floor roared their approval. When he said, "I alone can fix
> it," they shouted their approbation. The crowd peppered his speech
> with chants of "USA!" and "Lock her up!" and "Build the wall!"
> and "Trump!"[44]

Trump has also repeatedly expressed admiration for some of the world's most powerful dictators. He gushed admiration for the Chinese leader, Xi Jinping, when he was appointed effectively "President for Life." He called North Korea's Dear Leader, Kim Jong Un, a "talented" leader who can "run" his country "tough" and "loves his people," while Kim has starved and murdered thousands of his own people.[45]

While Trump has gone further than any recent president in his authoritarian rhetoric and policies, many prior presidents, including Nixon, have acted as if they, too, were above the law. The 1798 Alien and Sedition Acts, passed by Congress and signed by President John Adams, were four unconstitutional laws that limited freedom of speech, freedom of the press, and restricted activities of foreign residents. The 1917 Espionage Act and 1918 Sedition Act, passed at the urging of President Woodrow Wilson, banned many types of Constitutional free speech including:

> any disloyal, profane, scurrilous, or abusive language about the form of government of the United States . . . or the flag of the United States, or the uniform of the Army or Navy.[46]

The authoritarian turn has resurfaced virulently in the 21st century since 9/11. This goes well beyond the passing of the 2001 Patriot Act and Congressional authorization of any unilaterally declared presidential war deemed in pursuit of destroying terrorists. The longer-term trend has been the concentration of more and more executive power in the presidency and increased rule by executive orders, as seen under not just Trump but Presidents Ronald Reagan, George W. Bush and Barack Obama.

Charlie Savage, a *New York Times* reporter, has meticulously documented these trends in his books *Takeover*[47] and *Power Wars*.[48] Savage observes that a new view of permanent war since 9/11 changed the National Security state, turning the presidency into an emergency leader who could attack other countries without congressional consent, illegally imprison suspected Islamic jihadis, and refuse to carry out parts of congressionally passed laws that the President did not like. The rising "imperial president" could generally rule by his own executive orders and selective interpretation of the law, bypassing the democratic process.

In *Takeover*, focusing on George W. Bush and the "imperial Presidency," Savage focused attention on "signing statements." These were Presidential documents issued on the day of signing a law, where the president notes how they intend to implement legislation. Savage explains:

> I went back and read all these signing statements . . . since the beginning of the (W) Bush administration. What it turned out to be was a road map, essentially, to the implication of the unfettered presidency that Dick Cheney's legal team was trying to create . . . the hundreds of different laws that Bush had declared himself and the executive branch free to disobey.[49]

Savage observes that there was an explosion of signing statements under Bush signaling the rise of unconstitutional concentrated executive power:

> It was none of Congress' business what the government did, how it went about it what the limits of its conduct were. All these matters were solely for the president to decide. . . . The government existed to do what the president wanted it to do.[50]

In *Power Wars*, Savage documents how President Obama continued the Bush concentration of executive power:

> Barack Obama campaigned on changing George W. Bush's "global war on terror" but ended up entrenching extraordinary executive powers, from warrantless surveillance and indefinite detention to military commissions and targeted killings. Then Obama found himself bequeathing those authorities to Donald Trump. How did the United States get here? In *Power Wars*, Charlie Savage reveals high-level national security legal and policy deliberations in a way no one has done before. He tells inside stories of how Obama came to order the drone killing of an American citizen, preside

over an unprecedented crackdown on leaks, and keep a then-secret program that logged every American's phone calls.[51]

This is a history of rising authoritarianism, in which presidents, both Democratic and Republican, act like dictators in the name of national security and their Security stories. Trump, like Hitler, has taken this to a new level. While he has gained support from only about 40% of the population, the same that Hitler received before he became Chancellor, Trump is widely seen as the closest parallel to an American Dear Leader. Should he stay in office for a full one or two terms, and should the deep inequality between upstairs and downstairs continue to grow, we should remember Justice Louis Brandeis' warning:

> We must make our choice. We may have democracy, or we may have wealth concentrated in the hands of a few, but we can't have both.[52]

In Trump's future lies the possible loss of democracy and rise of the Dear Leader that Brandeis feared.

Follow Nature's Law of Brute Strength Over Weakness

Hitler was a culture warrior and believed that the shift to fascism was based on reading correctly the authoritarian psychology of the masses and building a culture of brute force. Merciless strength and willpower were the main moral virtues of fascist culture and weakness the greatest evil. We are seeing an American cultural movement seeking to intensify a culture of brute strength and violence, one with long roots in American history and institutions and representing a second great step toward fascism.

In our book, *Bully Nation*, we argued that militarized capitalism requires a culture of bullying, prizing power and violent force as dominant values. Trump, the most naked bully of US presidents, has helped empower and make respectable bullying behavior throughout American society. Our leading institutions create a fertile soil, with bullying endemic to both US global militarism and to a harsh US capitalism, that requires each person and each corporation to use whatever power possible to succeed. Racism in all its forms reinforces and intensifies these bullying tendencies. Trump, then, simply helps the nation take the second great step toward neo-fascism, enshrining more fully a culture of brute strength that has deep American roots.

In American capitalism, we have witnessed numerous forms of a war against workers, most recently as the Reagan revolution dismantled the New Deal. The unionized long-term worker is replaced by the temp or freelancer whose contract is like a "one-night stand." Workers lose good wages, job security, unions, medical plans and pensions. Senator Bernie Sanders vividly calls out corporations for their war on workers:

> It is unacceptable that the typical male worker made $783 less last year than he did 42 years ago.[53]

Sanders adds:

> Let us wage a moral and political war against the billionaires and corporate leaders, on Wall Street and elsewhere, whose policies and greed are destroying the Middle Class of America.[54]

This brutalization of corporate labor relations is tied to the political war of austerity to ensure that government spending goes to the military rather than to a "nanny" society that breeds an inherently weak citizenry. Capitalism can become fascist when it focuses on military spending and creates a culture of brute strength and toughness in the public. The fascist aim is to create a working population who submit to authority but have the willpower and combativeness to fight for itself, without unions or socialist handouts. The fascist state will kill off socialist parties and labor movements as undermining the culture of iron will in the populace.

These capitalist tendencies, which we describe in detail in *Bully Nation*, are tied to a culture of violence in a militarized society fighting permanent wars. With the military the most powerful and trusted institution, it is hardly surprising that violence and force become moral virtues. All soldiers are heroes who have learned to kill. Weakness is betrayal. The culture of violence has always pervaded the US, and we are now seeing a militarization of civil society, law enforcement and everyday life that incites violence of men against women, bosses against workers, whites against blacks, police against detainees, a culture defining fascist societies. Senator Rand Paul, a conservative Republican, is frank that Washington is encouraging and funding militarization of police:

> Washington has incentivized the militarization of local police precincts by using federal dollars to help municipal governments build what are essentially small armies—where police departments compete to acquire military gear that goes far beyond what most of Americans think of as law enforcement.[55]

The excessive violence and militarization of police and immigration border patrol (ICE) on the Mexican border are prime examples. "*I can't breathe*"—the cry of Michael Brown, an unarmed African-American male being strangled to death by police—symbolized the rising tide of police violence, in police forces increasingly armed with tanks and military-grade weapons. Similarly, the violence waged against Latino immigrants seeking asylum, when thousands of toddlers are forcibly removed from their parents and put in cages, when immigrants are shot trying to climb border fences or left to starve in desert crossing areas (where ICE officials have removed food and water bowls) are other signs of rising culturally approved institutional violence.

The militarization of schools is another example. As mass shootings occur more frequently, we are arming teachers, adding school security guards and building physical barriers and check-points. As schools become armed camps, the old problem of schoolyard bullies becomes intertwined with institutional violence melding the culture of education and the military. Schools may teach anti-bullying, a sign of the culture wars that divide the population around the morality of violence, but armed schools spread the message that force = safety = morality. This tacit enshrining of violence and toughness as moral virtues in schools, the workplace and other institutions helps define fascist societies.

The culture of violence among ordinary people is also telling. In the last chapter, we discussed the arming of America, as more people distrust and fear each other, and feel a need to "pack heat" to feel safe. Getting tough and placing a moral value on everyday aggression and violence—whether in road rage, competition for a place in a check-out line in stores, or simply among strangers or neighbors competing for parking places—is another sign of a shift toward a fascist way of life.[56] Consider the following example of road rage—one small example of an armed America getting out of control:

> Two women, aged thirty-four and forty, were driving home from work when one cut the other off on a congested highway. Their rage escalated as traffic crawled for miles and the women flashed their headlights and hit their brakes. Both vehicles left the interstate, heading for home. At the first traffic light, one woman left her car and approached the other, perhaps to the end the confrontation. The woman in the car shot the approaching woman in the face, killing her.[57]

The spread of this culture into politics is the defining mark of a full-scale shift to fascism. We have noted Trump's call to "rough up" and "throw out" protesters at his rallies, as well as the rise of Far Right and neo-Nazi violent groups spilling out into the streets in rallies that become violent and kill people, as in Charlottesville, Virginia in 2017. But we have not yet crossed the line into the fascist politics that sent Hitler's brown-shirted militias into the streets with guns blazing against Jews and other "domestic enemies." At that point, we will know that fascism is not fantasy.

Destroy the Foreign Enemy

In Chapter 3, we spelled out the Trump Security story that pours billions into modernizing nuclear weapons, fighting "radical Islamic terrorism" and keeping America strong against its foreign enemies. Rather than repeating this, we just want to briefly note that this third great step on the path to fascism—a sacred and full-time commitment to destroy the foreign enemy—has long been at the center of the American religion of "national security," officially sanctioned after World War II. The line between a state organized around national security and a fascist state can become blurry as enemies develop nukes, have capacities for nation-killing cyber-attacks and can threaten endless disruption that officials lump under the umbrella of terrorism.

Since World War II, destroying the umbrella enemies of Communism and then Islamic terrorism has moved to the center of American life. Permanent war against the "evil empire," as Reagan called the Soviet Union and then the "axis of evil," as Bush called Islamic "terrorist" nations, is filled with Orwellian possibilities. The greater the power and evil of the enemy, the greater the risk that "national security" can morph into authoritarianism and fascism.

Fascism is a national security state where the foreign threat is defined as so intense that it requires suspension of constitutional checks and balances—and of democracy itself. Two conditions can lead a democratic national security state in this direction. One involves the severity and evil of the enemy. The more evil that the threat is, the greater the possibility of a fascist turn. In the Obama Administration, images of ISIS decapitating a journalist created the kind of story of barbarism that fascism feeds on. George W. Bush's Vice-President, Dick Cheney, talked endlessly of the danger of nuclear terrorism, an even more barbaric threat, with Cheney suggesting an Islamic jihadi group could use nukes to wipe out US cities or Western civilization.

> I think the biggest strategic threat the United States faces today is the possibility of another 9/11 with a nuclear weapon or a biological agent of some kind. And I think al Qaeda is out there even as we meet, trying to figure out how to do that.[58]

The democratic national security state is most likely to sacrifice liberty and turn fascist in the pursuit of destroying an enemy that is so unimaginably catastrophic.

The second condition is the grip of the national security apparatus over the government and the culture. The more completely the state is devoted to national security—and to the extent the culture is focused on severe threats to personal survival from foreign enemies—the more that democracy is likely to take a fascist turn. This is intimately related to the first condition since the more evil or barbaric the enemy, the more fertile the soil for the national security religion to take over the culture and the state itself.

Since World War II, national security has been a dominant force in both US culture and politics. Elites have conjured up such evil enemies that the populace cannot feel secure without endlessly feeding the national security state. The military has become the most trusted national institution sucking up trillions of dollars annually. The national security umbrella provided by the Pentagon and soldiers turn them into America's only genuine heroes. Ironically, the national security state is so strong that anti-Trumpists, as noted in Chapter 3, have to legitimate themselves by denouncing him for weakening the FBI and CIA, the pillars of the security state. On the two most liberal and anti-Trumpist cable television channels, CNN and MSNBC, many commentators are former national security officials who legitimate anti-Trumpism by detailing the ways Trump is undermining the national security apparatus. Progressive hosts such as Rachel Maddow and Lawrence O'Donnell, journalists who are brilliant critics of Trump, nonetheless rarely give their own critique of the national security religion.

Meanwhile, the national security religion is being intensified by an intensified "border security" Security story and the demonization of undocumented immigrants. Having long called them "rapists" and "criminals," as noted earlier, Trump then declared crossers "invaders" and in June, 2018, repeatedly called for "summary deportations" of immigrants crossing the borders:

> Donald Trump on Monday again issued a call to deprive undocumented immigrants of their right to due process, arguing that people trying to cross the border should be summarily deported without a trial or an appearance before a judge.[59]

Trump also proclaimed that the suspension of rights

Is the only real answer.[60]

This is the sort of rhetoric and policy that could take the national security state a few further big steps toward embrace of fascism, supported by a terrified population. The same could be true of a disabling cyber-attack on our national grid or a terrorist attack that destroyed an American city. The religion of the security state is already so powerful that any such major new attack could cement the shift toward a declaration of emergency leading to fascism. The events of 9/11 moved us partly down that path; a second 9/11 might finish the job.

Destroy the Domestic Enemy

Destroying the domestic enemy is the fourth great step to fascism. Exterminating the Jewish enemy in Germany was a centerpiece of Hitler's fascist Security story. So was the abolition of labor unions, socialist and Communist parties and movements.

In the last chapter we discussed in some detail the Reagan/Trumpist/Republican war against minorities, gays and women, secular liberal bi-coastal elites, trade unions and Left-leading parties and social movements, all seen as domestic enemies in the US Security story reigning at least since Reagan. The question here is when and if this war will take the US toward fascism? As with the foreign enemy, this happens when the domestic enemies are demonized and dehumanized, portrayed in the Security story as so dangerous that they must be exterminated, banned or imprisoned. If you want fascism, do what Hitler did with the Jew: make him the anti-Christ.

This extreme dehumanization might seem more difficult to do with domestic US enemies than foreign ones, but the opposite can be the case. Domestic enemies are already inside the country so they are a more visible threat, perhaps the neighbor next door. They have the right as US citizens to vote their own alien agenda and party or movement into power. Most importantly, the war with the domestic enemy, since it is so entangled with culture wars, is deeply emotional and spiritual, involving issues of identity and God. When you fight about God, the enemy can quickly become the anti-Christ and trigger a shift toward fascism.

In the US, fighting the domestic enemy involves revving up the culture wars that are already intense and deeply emotional. They unite religious, rural and culturally conservative workers downstairs with capitalist conservative elites upstairs. As they fight liberal and Left professionals and workers who are also trying to unite upstairs and downstairs, the risks of class war that could topple the upstairs/downstairs system fade away. The culture wars shift social conflict safely away from the issues of capitalism and economic inequality toward explosive issues of immigration, race, gender, family values and other cultural issues at the heart of national identity and fascism.

The US has had its culture wars for decades without fascism, although the Civil War, a war about slavery, can be seen as part of a struggle between democratic and fascist capitalism. Nonetheless, despite the long legacy of violence against African-Americans, other people of color and workers, American culture wars, since the Civil War, have not led to fascism. But the potential is stronger than it might appear, because culture wars have often been on the brink of what Harvard political scientist, Samuel Huntington, called, "Clashes of civilization."[61] When that happens, and culture wars become all-out civilizational warfare, the fourth great step toward fascism has begun.

Fascism can be defined as a culture war inflamed into civilizational war about national identity and God. Hitler turned the Jewish domestic enemy into the most dangerous racial and cultural threat to Germany identity and Christianity. As culture wars turn into civilizational crusades to protect God and the nation—by eliminating the cultural enemy across the street or the next state over—democratic culture wars are moving toward fascism. Might a culture war fought by Christian white nationalists become like Hitler's war fought by Aryan white nationalists? Richard Spencer, one of the most prominent American white nationalist leaders, sees Trump as championing a white cultural war to take back the country:

> Trump has opened the door to nationalism in this country—not American nationalism but the white race. Once that door has fully swung open, you can't close it.[62]

Spencer also has said in a speech at Texas A&M:

> This country does belong to white people, culturally, politically, socially, everything. We defined what America is.[63]

Huntington argues that civilizations are the foundation of personal and national identity. Who am I, he argues, is the most important question we each face. Our civilization gives us the answer; it tells us what we can wear, what we can eat, how to be a good man or women, what work is worth doing, what kind of government we need, what values we should cherish and what God we should worship. If our civilization is under attack, we will defend it with every ounce of our being, because our core identity and way of life is on the line.

Culture wars are emotional and can become even genocidal because our identity is at stake. If our Security story tells us that those on the other side of the culture wars are defaming or ripping apart our civilization—our morality and God—many will join a violent fight to exterminate those on the other side of the cultural divide. They are dishonoring us personally as well as the nation. When leaders call for all-out destruction of the cultural enemy at home, with violence an acceptable tool, fascism is nearing.

Such appeals have grown under President Trump, who has taken brutally violent measures against undocumented immigrants and their kids, young Black men and almost all minority communities, and the more than two million prisoners in US jails. Immigration is the tip of his spear in a violent culture war pointing toward an American fascism, empowering actual neo-Nazi hate groups and allied white supremacists. Here is Richard Spencer again:

> Immigration is a kind of proxy war—and maybe a last stand—for White Americans who are undergoing a painful recognition that, unless dramatic action is taken, their grandchildren will live in a country that is alien and hostile.[64]

Trump is clearly empowering Spencer and other white supremacists who are waging a culture war, turned Huntingtonian civilizational war:

> The ideal of a white ethno-state—and it is an ideal—is something that I think we should think about in the sense of what could come after America, . . . It's kind of like a grand goal. . . . It's a way

of thinking about [how] we want a new type of society that would actually be a homeland for all white people.[65]

Some of Trump's leading advisors as well as followers have also denounced American Muslims as incapable of being true Americans, much as Hitler saw Jews as incapable of being true Germans. Trump has also called for imprisoning Hillary Clinton, his presidential rival, urged supporters to rough up protesters and proposed new libel laws and even shut down of the "fake news" mass media. He is ginning up our culture divide as a clash of civilization requiring violence and extra-constitutional emergency measures that have the smell of fascism.

But this inflaming of the culture wars did not begin with Trump nor will it end with him. In the post-World War II era, during the Watergate era, President Nixon called for the "silent majority" to save the nation from the "anti-American" activists of the 1960s. In the early 1970s, corporate elites funded the New Right and organized Christian evangelicals to save the white Christian nation that was under existential threat from secular socialist liberals and Black revolutionaries. This was enshrined in the politics of the Reagan revolution, as Reagan, and his southern strategist, Lee Atwater, used culture wars to attack secular liberals and Blacks as criminals or traitors uniting to destroy American civilization and God. Stefan Forbes, who made a film, *Boogie Man*, about Atwater's pioneering role in the Reagan revolution to exploit culture wars about domestic enemies and fearful enemies, said this in a revealing interview with BuzzFlash:

BuzzFlash: *It seemed that Atwater and Rove were most skillful at using fear that burrows into our primitive emotions to win elections. Have we outgrown this as a nation, or is it just taking a breather in the swamp land?*

Stefan Forbes: *I've been asked that a lot, especially since late October, when it became clear Obama was redrawing our electoral map and redefining the role of race in American politics. But ending fear in politics is kind of a tall order, isn't it? Human beings are hardwired for fear. The fight-or-flight syndrome is an essential part of how we learned to survive. Atwater understood this on a gut level.*[66]

Atwater had led the Republican Party in how to get white conservatives to hate and fear Blacks and liberals so much they would wage civilizational war. Bush and Dick Cheney picked up the civilizational war theme, arguing that the liberal and Left culture warriors, tied to minorities, immigrants and Muslims, were all "terrorists" who were the most frightening of all civilizational enemies because they embodied pure barbarism.

As Trump has consolidated his base around his own civilizational war, we have moved beyond a deep partisan divide into a civil war around basic values, with the president leading a charge against the rule of law and the Constitution itself. His base is only at most 40–43% of Americans but Hitler also never got above that amount of electoral support himself. Hitler mobilized that base into an armed minority successfully challenging democracy and embracing fascism. We should not minimize the possibility that Trump—or some successor—could do the same.

5

THE FAILINGS OF THE AMERICAN LEFT

HOW TO BE YOUR OWN WORST ENEMY

What good is having the right to sit at a lunch counter
If you can't afford to buy a hamburger?
—Martin Luther King Jr.

I actually think it is people like myself who have been fighting for
our rights to free speech and I would like the right to defend my
own right to free speech, not have soldiers doing it for me. I don't
think I need soldiers.
—Medea Benjamin

Because the Security story is so dangerous, we need a new national narrative. The dangers have become gut-wrenching since President Trump was elected, leading to mass resistance that we haven't seen since the 1960s.[1] The Women's March, on the day after Trump was inaugurated, was the biggest protest in world history. It was followed by mass marches against Trump's Muslim travel ban and his immigration "zero tolerance" policy at the border that led to thousands of kids separated from their parents and caged in old Walmart warehouses and military bases.

Many other movements erupted, including the "Never Again" student protests after the Parkland mass shootings, the #MeToo movement by women against sexual violence, the teachers' and nurses' strikes for more pay not just for themselves but for their students and schools, the Black Lives Matter protests against mass incarceration and police violence and the Indivisible movement to elect progressives to Congress. Fifty years after Bobby Kennedy was killed, it was if his voice was resonating from the grave:

> Each time a man stands up for an ideal, or acts to improve the lot of others, or strikes out against injustice, he sends out a tiny ripple of hope, and crossing each other from a million different centers of energy and daring, those ripples build a current that can sweep down the mightiest wall of oppression.[2]

Kennedy said this in 1966 in South Africa, while joining the resistance to Apartheid. The ripple of Resistance movements at this writing is a rejection not just of Trump personally, but of the policies of the capitalist aristocrats he serves: his vast military spending, his huge tax cuts for the rich, his anti-unionism, his deep cuts in social welfare spending and his financial and environmental deregulation benefiting big banks and oil and gas companies. This is a plethora of nationalist economic, racial and state violence arising out of a Security story that is all about protecting the power of the 1% upstairs and the ruling capitalist system.

The "Resistance" suggests the stirring of a progressive community that could change the national story of fear and the militarized capitalism that it protects in the name of security. It as if millions of Americans suddenly discovered the wisdom of Mark Twain who observed:

> Courage is resistance to fear, mastery of fear, not absence of fear.[3]

The Left broadly conceived—including liberals, progressives, the Democratic Party and socialist or other Left movements on the streets— is the natural political vehicle for changing the narrative. Nationalism and capitalism are both ideologies historically associated with the Right and its Security story. But concepts of Left and Right are changing— with Trump and Bernie Sanders sharing certain populist voters. The new national narrative that we need is a tale of universal security—appealing to people on all sides of the political spectrum—in the spirit of democracy and universal rights.

The capitalist Security story is fundamentally a nationalist ideology. It celebrates the nation state, unites its upstairs and downstairs, and saves it from endless enemies, real and invented. It diverts popular anger from the billionaires to endless enemies abroad and at home.

Since Trump's election, the Security story has become a tale of white nationalism, the cultural narrative that Trump and Steve Bannon, his first chief advisor, have tacitly supported. It is still a capitalist story protecting global corporate interests like those of Trump himself, but it exploits racialized nationalist symbols and headlines. White nationalists organized and celebrated the Unite the Right neo-Nazi march in Charlottesville, Virginia, August 14, 2017, in which a neo-Nazi killed one woman and marchers chanted the Nazi slogan, "Blood and Soil," and wore swastikas. Trump endorsed some of the organizers in this infamous phrase:

You also had some very fine people on both sides.[4]

But long before Trump said these words that will echo through history for their barely disguised neo-Nazi praise, the US Security story has been nationalist, with strong racial elements. To protect capitalist globalism, Trump has simply written another draft of the story of the nation and national security that has been triumphant for most of American history.

Progressives and the Left have long been skeptical of nationalism, especially the jingoistic and militarist form enshrined in the American Security story. As we have seen, the story benefits the 1%, an ideology aimed at uniting downstairs American workers with American corporations while also promoting unjust wars against manufactured enemies. The Left has leaned toward internationalism, seeking global solidarity based on universal rights spelled out in the 1948 UN Declaration of Human Rights. It was Henry Wallace, Franklin D. Roosevelt's Vice President, the most progressive figure ever to hold such a high office in the US, who championed international solidarity, including early efforts to build friendship between the US and the USSR to avert a Cold War after World War II. And it was Eleanor Roosevelt, one of the most leftist figures in the left-leaning New Deal, who was the most important architect of the 1948 UN Declaration. It is fundamentally progressive and clearly critical of both nationalism and capitalism in its embrace of universal rights to equality and social welfare. Some key articles include global rights to shelter, food, education, health care and good jobs—key elements of true security:

Article 22.

Everyone, as a member of society, has the right to social security and is entitled to realization, through national effort and international co-operation and in accordance with the organization and resources of each State, of the economic, social and cultural rights indispensable for his dignity and the free development of his personality.

Article 23.

1. *Everyone has the right to work, to free choice of employment, to just and favorable conditions of work and to protection against unemployment.*
2. *Everyone, without any discrimination, has the right to equal pay for equal work.*
3. *Everyone who works has the right to just and favorable remuneration ensuring for himself and his family an existence worthy of human dignity, and supplemented, if necessary, by other means of social protection.*
4. *Everyone has the right to form and to join trade unions for the protection of his interests.*

Article 24.

Everyone has the right to rest and leisure, including reasonable limitation of working hours and periodic holidays with pay.

Article 25.

1. *Everyone has the right to a standard of living adequate for the health and wellbeing of himself and of his family, including food, clothing,*

housing and medical care and necessary social services, and the right to
security in the event of unemployment, sickness, disability, widowhood,
old age or other lack of livelihood in circumstances beyond his control.

The UN Declaration is something like a global constitution for universal and true security. The Left has also always been the main champion of reforming or transforming the upstairs/downstairs capitalist house to secure universal rights and security. Its security story moves away from the narrow and militarized focus on national security to a story about how to protect the universal human rights of all Americans—and all citizens of the world—for economic, social and environmental security. It's the kind of story that Bernie Sanders appeared to endorse in his support of "democratic socialism."

But despite the rise of "the Resistance," the popularity of Sanders and the growing critique of the 1% American capitalism, progressives and the Left have not, at this writing, been successful in creating a new national narrative in the spirit of the UN Declaration. In this chapter, we will explain these failures, which need to be remedied if liberals and the Left are to offer a new story of universal and true security and change our militarized capitalism house.

Failings of Progressives and the Left

The weakness of US liberals and the Left is obvious when we look at the US political landscape. At this writing, in 2018, a deeply conservative Republican Party controls all branches of the American government. This includes the White House, the Senate and the House, the Supreme Court, and the majority of state governors and legislatures. Moreover, starting with the Clinton Administration, the Democratic Party abandoned the social democratic and progressivism of Franklin D. Roosevelt and the New Deal, becoming again a second party of business that it had been before the New Deal. Bill Clinton made alliances with Wall Street, choosing Wall Street titan, Robert Rubin, CEO of Citibank, as his Treasury Secretary and accepting big donations from big business, a practice followed by Hillary Clinton in her 2016 run against Trump. At the time of George W. Bush, many said there were just two mainstream parties in the US, both corporate: Bush and Bush Lite, but this was not new; business interests had dominated in the Democratic presidencies of Woodrow Wilson, Harry Truman, JFK, Lyndon Johnson and Jimmy Carter.

The Right has been in power since the 1980 Reagan revolution, which created a domestic "regime change," enshrining a new Gilded Age of corporate aristocratic rule.[5] What we have elsewhere called the "Third Corporate Regime"—with the 1890s Gilded Age the First Corporate Regime and the Roaring 1920s the Second Corporate Regime—has this birth certificate.

Name: Third Corporate Regime
Date of Birth: Election Day, 1980
Father: Ronald Reagan
Mother: Corporate America
Headquarters: Washington D. C.
Brief Biography: The regime is almost 40 years old. It took form under the Reagan Administration. The regime consolidated itself under Bush I, secured legitimacy from Democrats under President Clinton, and intensified itself under Bush II. President Obama sought mild reforms within the regime and President Trump has taken it toward greater authoritarianism. The aim of the regime is to shift sovereignty from citizens to transnational corporations and to transform government into a business partner committed to maximizing global profits for a small number of global executives and shareholders. It is showing signs of age and is viewed by much of the world as dangerous.
Caution is advised: Registry of Regimes, Washington D.C.[6]

Since the birth of this corporate regime, the Left and the Democratic Party have been in deep decline. Under President Clinton, the Democrats bought into corporate rule and global militarism in the name of security. The broader liberal and Left community shifted from class politics to identity politics, as discussed shortly.

The mainstream media has created the impression that cultural and political differences make the 2010s the most polarized time ever in America, but this is untrue. In the 1860s, there was a literal civil war. The

"New Left" of the 1960s/1970s was way to the left of what is now called Left and the Right became more entrenched in response. What has changed is that there is more discord within the halls of Congress. Up until the Reagan era, Democrats and Republicans would routinely go out to dinner together. The Democrats have actually moved rightward, but the Republicans have moved so far right that they hardly speak the same language. However, the differences within the general population are dwarfed in comparison to what they were 40 years ago.

American politics has become a new contest between the corporate Right and the Far Right, with the Left largely out of the picture. The rise from the swamps of white supremacist, anti-immigrant and neo-Nazi groups, as well as gun groups, white nationalists and the alt-Right, is challenging the Establishment Right. They want to oust the traditional leadership of the Republican Party, other than President Trump, and they embrace the wildly authoritarian Security story Trump tweets and enacts. Many pundits argued that by 2018, Trump had successfully pulled off a "hostile takeover" of the Republican Party, an exaggeration since Trump has enacted most of the Reagan Republican policy and is largely embracing the Third Corporate Regime. It is true, though, that Trump is more nakedly authoritarian, racist and anti-immigrant—and more hyper-nationalist. All this could be interpreted as meaning that the main political game in town at this writing in 2018, is between the Right and the Far Right, though both have their own very similar Security stories whipping up fear of enemies abroad and at home.

Moreover, the culture wars—led on the Right by Evangelical Christians, anti-abortionists, anti-immigrant groups, racists, champions of "family values" and other advocates of traditional culture—are on the ascendancy. The Left has not done a good job of pointing out that it is the real defender of family values with its support for paid parental leaves and publicly funded child care, policies which Republicans oppose. The Far Right is Trump's base, and while they have always been a force in America, Trump has empowered them with a White House platform. Here's Trump, while separating Central American kids from their parents at the border, tweeting about the Democratic Party and immigrants "infesting" America, language the Far Right loves, since it suggests an almost neo-Nazi purge:

"Democrats are the problem. They don't care about crime and want illegal immigrants, no matter how bad they may be, to pour into and infest our Country, like MS-13," Mr. Trump tweeted. "They can't win on their terrible policies, so they view them as potential voters!"[7]

With Trump's help, the culture wars are bringing out of the back-woods a Far Right that is so far right that it is even troubling corporate elites who have long been conservative and Republican. Most of the corporate 1% embrace the Trumpian Security story that could lead not just to white nationalism, but to a new American fascism, as discussed in the last chapter.

This does not mean that there are not major progressive or "left" sectors of the US population. President Trump never gained a major-ity support of American voters, supported only by a highly mobilized Republican base of about 40% of the nation. Moreover, based on many years of public opinion polling from Pew, Gallup and other leading poll-sters, majorities of Americans are progressive or "Left" on most issues, as summarized in 2017 by sociologist Peter Dreier:

The Economy

- *82% of Americans think wealthy people have too much power and influ-ence in Washington.*
- *69% think large businesses have too much power and influence in Washington.*
- *78% of likely voters support stronger rules and enforcement on the finan-cial industry.*

Inequality

- *82% of Americans think economic inequality is a "very big" (48%) or "moderately big" (34%) problem. Even 69% of Republicans share this view.*
- *59% of registered voters—and 51% of Republicans—favor raising the maximum amount that low-wage workers can make and still be eligible for the Earned Income Tax Credit, from $14,820 to $18,000.*

Money in Politics

- *96% of Americans—including 96% of Republicans—believe money in politics is to blame for the dysfunction of the US political system.*
- *78% of Americans say we need sweeping new laws to reduce the influence of money in politics.*
- *73% of registered voters have an unfavorable opinion of the Supreme Court's Citizens United decision.*

Taxes

- *76% believe the wealthiest Americans should pay higher taxes.*

Minimum Wage

- *59% favor raising the federal minimum wage to $12 an hour.*
- *48% support raising the national minimum wage to $15 an hour. (A survey of registered voters found that 54% favored a $15 minimum wage.)*

Workers' Rights

- *61% of Americans—including 42% of Republicans—approve of labor unions.*
- *74% of registered voters—including 71% of Republicans—support requiring employers to offer paid parental and medical leave.*

Health Care

- *60% of Americans believe "it is the federal government's responsibility to make sure all Americans have healthcare coverage."*
- *60% of registered voters favor "expanding Medicare to provide health insurance to every American."*

Education

- *63% of registered voters—including 47% of Republicans—of Americans favor making four-year public colleges and universities tuition-free.*
- *59% of Americans favor free early-childhood education.*

Climate Change and the Environment

- *76% of voters are "very concerned" or "somewhat concerned" about climate change.*
- *72% of voters think it is a "bad idea" to cut funding for scientific research on the environment and climate change.*

Gun Safety

- *84% of Americans support requiring background checks for all gun buyers.*
- *77% of gun owners support requiring background checks for all gun buyers.*

Criminal Justice

- *57% of Americans believe police officers generally treat Blacks and other minorities differently than they treat whites.*
- *60% of Americans believe the recent killings of Black men by police are part of a broader pattern of how police treat Black Americans (compared with 39% who believe they are isolated incidents).*

Immigration

- *68% of Americans—including 48% of Republicans—believe the country's openness to people from around the world "is essential to who we are as a nation." Just 29% say that "if America is too open to people from all over the world, we risk losing our identity as a nation."*
- *76% of registered voters—including 69% of Republicans—support allowing undocumented immigrants brought to the country as children (Dreamers) to stay in the country.*

Abortion and Women's Health

- *58% of Americans believe that abortion should be legal in all or most cases.*
- *68% of Americans—including 54% of Republicans—support the requirement for private health insurance plans to cover the full cost of birth control.*[8]

This strikingly progressive public opinion profile helps explain why the majority of Americans are fiercely opposed to Donald Trump. It also helps explain the rise of Bernie Sanders, Elizabeth Warren and other Democratic Party leaders, reflecting the shift of the Democratic base and Independents in a more progressive direction.

Moreover, the Resistance was just the most recent outcropping of progressive and overtly Left social movements that have been on the scene since the end of the 1960s. These include today Black Lives Matter, gay rights movements, feminist movements for equal pay and now #MeToo, anti-climate change movements such as 350.org, Our Revolution espousing the "democratic socialism" of Bernie Sanders and numerous others. By some counts, including a detailed enumeration by Paul Hawken in his best-seller, *Blessed Unrest*, there are hundreds of thousands of grassroots movements and both local and national organizations devoted to anti-racism, feminism, civil rights, immigrant rights, labor rights, animal rights, social justice, peace and stopping climate change and saving the environment.[9]

Nonetheless, the progressive communities are politically weak and the very existence of what might be called a Left is now in question. While election of a Democratic Congress could limit Trump's power, it will not change the underlying problem. This reflects deep changes in the idea of what it means to be progressive or "Left," as well as serious problems in the organization of liberal and Left groups and their ability to mobilize the electoral support of much of the population, including downstairs workers and poor people of all races and genders who should be their fervent base.

Failing the Class Question

The question of whether a Left still exists in the US is a real issue. Historically, the Left has always been focused on the capitalist system. Leftist analysis was a critique of a society built around classes, and an examination of how the capitalist class exploited workers for profit. The Left treated capitalism as the root cause of many other leading social problems, especially militarism and racism, and argued that to achieve a just society one would have to move beyond capitalism to advance universal human rights and subordinate markets and profits to human needs.

The US has an important but largely ignored history of a populist and progressive Left driving an American debate about capitalism. In the 1890s Gilded Age, the populists formed a People's Party that advocated for nationalization of Wall Street and worker co-ops. Socialists in World War I, such as Eugene Debs, who headed a socialist party and won 919,799 votes for president while in jail for opposing World War I, also put the issue of capitalism into the national conversation. He was imprisoned when he observed:

> The working class who fight all the battles, the working class who make the supreme sacrifices, the working class who freely shed their blood and furnish the corpses, have never yet had a voice in either declaring war or making peace. It is the ruling class that invariably does both. They alone declare war and they alone make peace.[10]

In the New Deal, millions of New Deal liberals, socialists and Communists sought to organize workers to create a strong working-class countervailing power to the corporations, with many demanding an American socialism. In the 1960s, a mass Left emerged which fought not just for civil rights and against the Vietnam war, but developed a serious critique of capitalism, arguing for socialism and participatory democracy. The 1960s Left linked racism and militarism to capitalism, as did Martin Luther King in his final years, dying for the cause of sanitation workers in Memphis. A year before his murder, King said in a speech:

> The evils of capitalism are as real as the evils of militarism and evils of racism.[11]

A few months later King expanded this focus on capitalism:

> There are forty million poor people here, and one day we must ask the question, "Why are there forty million poor people in

America?" And when you begin to ask that question, you are raising a question about the economic system, about a broader distribution of wealth. When you ask that question, you begin to question the capitalistic economy.[12]

But since 1980, intimidated by the Reagan revolution, the progressives and the Left stopped asking this question and profoundly changed their nature and vision. They moved away from a critique of capitalism and evolved into siloed identity movements focused on race, gender, sexual orientation and ethnicity. Some might conclude that militarized capitalist is just fine. We need only to change the race and gender of the people at the top of capitalist institutions. The Simpsons parodied that attitude:

> The Left (speaking with picture of Karl Marx in the background): We now live in a world where the richest 8 men own more than the poorest 3.6 billion.

> "Liberals" (Lisa Simpson in the audience) That's an outrage! At least 4 of them should be women of color.[13]

Racism, sexism and other identity themes are obviously critical political issues. But they need to be organized in class-conscious ways, together with labor movements, to see how capitalism breeds many of their shared problems and how they can be overcome together.

By the 1980s, though, the question of capitalism was largely off the table. This was an epic transformation, since it opened the door to the Right to lead the conversation about our economic system and advance a unifying agenda around nationalism. As the Left—and the Democratic Party—focused on racism and sexism, the Right were the ones speaking to workers, raising their own universalizing ideas about how love of nation unites American workers and capitalists. With the Reagan revolution in 1980, the progressive and Left critique of capitalism had largely disappeared from the public conversation, and white workers increasingly became "Reagan Democrats," former members of the Democratic Party who shifted to the Republican ticket.

Since the 1980s, the question of capitalism has all but vanished from public and even progressive debate. Race and gender have become the leading progressive and Left issues. Many Black and female activists have tried to talk about this as a serious problem in their own movements, including an African-American community organizer:

> As an elder shaped by my time in the Black Freedom struggle, I have to say . . . we need to deal with the lack of clarity and analysis around the role of capitalism. It's so often the big elephant in the room. People are organizing around labor, immigration, and all kinds of stuff but they are not talking about capitalism enough. It shows up in the limits of what we come up with and what people can imagine. It's like driving with a GPS but not knowing where you are driving to. People are driving in circles—around strategy, resources, etc.—because they are not clear about their destination.[14]

This public silence about capitalism opened the door to Trump, since he alone focused on big problems in trade and global capitalism that hurt American workers. As the Democratic Party and the Left focused on other more culturally divisive questions, it is hardly surprising that Trump could attract workers with an anti-globalist economic message and a nationalist Security story that offered both jobs and cultural self-respect to "forgotten" American workers. It remains unclear that we can now speak of an American Left in the historical sense, since the Left too became absorbed with identity politics and no longer was a force for creating a national conversation about militarized capitalism that could unify most people who were disempowered in the capitalist house, the conversation that was what made the Left the Left.

Without that conversation, it is very hard to understand and change the Security story. Its aim is to keep the upstairs and the downstairs of the capitalist house united, diverting the anger of workers away from corporate elite and instead creating a capitalist-worker alliance against the enemies of the capitalist house, including the PMC social welfare and service branches of the state itself. But without a conversation about capitalism, we lack context for understanding why the Security story is an irrational and harmful tool to justify the existence of both upstairs and downstairs, to obscure the conflict that would rationally drive the downstairs against the upstairs, and to show how nationalism manufactures enemies to unite groups that are in an exploitative relation within capitalism. Put simply, without a progressivism or Left focused on capitalism, capitalism is safe. The 1% will increase its fortunes as the downstairs decline, and the real enemies bred by capitalism—climate change, militarism and extreme inequality and poverty endemic to capitalism itself—will be ignored as we fight the enemies we have manufactured.

The Failings of Identity Politics

As progressives and the Left have dissolved into a "class-less" identity politics, they have unwittingly reinforced capitalism and its Security story. Identity politics, just like the capitalist Security story, divides the population by culture rather than class. As progressives and the Left pursue identity agendas without a strong class consciousness, they join the Right in splitting working people by race, gender and sexual orientation, as well as by cultural values such as religion. Anti-racist and feminist movements are crucially important, but when they lack class consciousness, they can reinforce the tribalism that fuels the Right and sustains capitalism, while dividing and weakening identity groups that have far more in common than they realize.

They also create the illusion that the militaristic capitalism works, that formerly oppressed peoples are now being given a "piece of the pie" with no critique of the pie. That the Smithsonian now acknowledges African-American history with its own museum is something to applaud. However, inside the museum is a pyramid recognizing capitalists who have donated hundreds of thousands or more. The top tier of the pyramid is for someone who gave over $20,000,000. It has only one name: Oprah Winfrey.

Magrass witnessed this:

> The day the museum opened there was a gala banquet celebrating the event. Blacks in tuxedoes, evening gowns, gold, diamonds and pearls entered through the museum gate. On the other side of the gate were rows of homeless Blacks.

In their current form, identity groups—now the core of progressive politics and the Left—can become like other capitalist special interests. They promote their own group's concerns—breaking the glass ceiling while trying to move into elite groups—while not questioning whether those elites should exist. This not only reinforces capitalism but turns identity struggles into a self-interested politics going against the grain of progressivism. Cheryl Sandberg, COO of Facebook, called women to "lean in" to the corporation and fight to get into the corner office, leading a kind of corporate feminism. The feminist and gay rights movements have come to demand that the military become more "open," that it should admit women, gays and transgender people into equal opportunity body bags, but the Left of the 1960/1970s questioned if the military should exist, period. As one gay feminist has written insightfully:

> Do we really want equal access to death, mayhem and destruction? Do we really want an equal opportunity to kill and be killed? Do we really want an equal shot at coming home in a body bag? Is that the kind of equality we are fighting for, not our right to love but our right to die and our right to kill? . . . There was a time, in the 60s, when most young folk, of all sexual persuasions were anti-war. . . . I remember a time when a much larger number of lesbians and gays were radicals. We didn't just want equality for ourselves. We were multi-issue, not single issue. We fought for equality for people of color. We fought against racism, anti-Semitism and sexism. We had a feminist analysis of the world, including the war machine. . . . Be sure to look for my next 10–15 articles on why women should be banned from the military, why African Americans, Arabs, Jews, transgender folks, bisexuals, young people, progressives, immigrants, both documented and undocumented, poor people as well as straight white Christians, upper class and wealthy men should all be banned from the military.

> Equal access for all? No: No access for anyone. Discriminate against everyone. Ban everyone from serving in the military. Shut the military down. No one should be allowed to kill and die. Amen.[15]

Is a militaristic capitalism changed only by accepting more Blacks and women upstairs and keeping most other people—Black, brown, women especially—downstairs the goal of the Left? The progressive values of Left identity politics suggest otherwise but we would need a conversation about capitalism to bring this home, essentially a reintegration of identity politics with class politics. This is precisely what Martin Luther King began to advocate at the time he was killed—and he was murdered partly because of his awakening consciousness about capitalism. In 1967, a year before his murder and in a challenge to "class-less" identity politics, King expanded on the theme that "the evils of racism, economic exploitation and militarism are all tied together."

You can't really get rid of one without getting rid of the others.[16]

When identity politics abandons universalizing themes and reinforces tribalism, it disposes people toward fear and belief in the enemies manufactured by the upstairs elites, while weakening anti-racist and feminist movements. Workers of different races and genders are more easily turned against each other despite the economic and social interests they share. This is contrary to the underlying values of progressivism—in fact, it destroys the historic universalism of the Left—and promotes the nationalism that feeds off of fear of enemies.

Failing to Debunk Manufactured Enemies
Many progressives have bought into the national security religion at the center of the Security story. This includes anti-Trumpists on liberal cable television channels such as CNN and MSNBC, who reflexively treat Russia as a hostile power, with journalists as liberal and smart as Rachel Maddow obsessed with Russia's evils and threats to the US and world. True, Russian meddling in the 2016 elections and possible collusion with the Trump campaign is an extremely serious problem. But Maddow and other liberal journalists are helping fuel the New Cold War that the US foreign policy establishment and national security apparatus have been working hard to restart. The Progressive media group FAIR is organizing to challenge MSNBC's liberalism that is feverishly anti-Russian:

MSNBC's incessant "Russiagate" coverage has put the network at the media forefront of overheated hyperbole about the Kremlin. And continually piling up the dry tinder of hostility toward Russia boosts the odds of a cataclysmic blowup between the world's two nuclear superpowers.[17]

Independent journalist Robert Parry has made the same critique:

to even suggest that there is another side to the story makes you a "Putin apologist" or "Kremlin stooge." Western journalists now apparently see it as their patriotic duty to hide key facts that otherwise would undermine the demonizing of Putin and Russia. Ironically, many "liberals" who cut their teeth on skepticism about the Cold War and the bogus justifications for the Vietnam War now insist that we must all accept whatever the U.S. intelligence community feeds us, even if we're told to accept the assertions on faith.[18]

Russia should be sanctioned for its interference with US elections, but that does not justify taking for granted the Establishment's view that Russia is the principal threat to the US or the world. This is the view that the Bush Administration took of Saddam's Iraq: Saddam was a dictator but he never should have been treated as the global "face of evil" and great enemy that was used to justify invading Iraq and creating regime change.

The problem here is that liberals and progressives so often treat the US as the defender of freedom, fighting mercilessly "enemies" that it has helped create through its own militarism and imperialism. The US invasion of Iran in 1953 and overthrow of its democratically elected president, Mohammed Mossadegh, led to the horrors of the US-sponsored Shah rule, with the Shah torturing and jailing millions of his own citizens, aided by US funding. This led to the revolution putting the Ayatollah and hardline clergy in power, calling for "Death to America." This was a perfect case of how US policy created its own "enemy," but it is rarely discussed even in the liberal press.

The 2003 US invasion of Iraq and overthrow of Saddam helped create or increase the influence of its own new greatest enemies: ISIS, Assad's Syria and Iran. Noam Chomsky argues this forcefully regarding ISIS:

> ISIS is a monstrosity. There's not much doubt about that. It didn't come from nowhere. It's one of the results of the U.S. hitting a very vulnerable society—Iraq—with a sledgehammer, which elicited sectarian conflicts that had not existed. They became very violent. The U.S. violence made it worse. We're all familiar with the crimes. Out of this came lots of violent, murderous forces. ISIS is one.[19]

Similarly, decades of US intervention and brutal wars in Central and Latin America have created "enemies" throughout the region. A global hegemon such as the US has been waging *savage* wars and bullying other nations for decades, ensuring that they will defend themselves and resent the US in ways that the Security story can then label them as foreign enemies. But they are enemies the US created by its own superpower agenda of dominance, and any truly progressive voice would be explaining this over and over to the US public, rather than allowing the Security story to label victims of US aggression our enemies. They have every reason to fear the US and defend themselves against it. If they are enemies, it is because the US turned them into our fearful and angry foes. Nabeel Khoury, a former US deputy chief of mission in Yemen, argues that:

> Drone strikes take out a few bad guys to be sure, but they also kill a large number of innocent civilians. Given Yemen's tribal structure, the U.S. generates roughly forty to sixty new enemies for every AQAP [al Qaeda in the Arabian Peninsula] operative killed by drones.[20]

But not only do liberal media and Democratic party progressives not tell the story of US hegemony that Americans need to hear, but the peace movements on the streets in large numbers in the 1960s have largely disappeared, meaning that even the Left has failed to educate the US public on hegemonic US foreign policy.

After Trump was elected, liberals attacked him for questioning the integrity of security institutions like the CIA and the FBI, agents which the Left used to consider fundamentally illegitimate.

> Back then, for example, the CIA was understood as a nest of liars and psychopaths who toppled democratically chosen leaders, lied to the public to start wars, and ran sick experiments on innocents using drugs and mind control techniques. . . . These days, however, with Trump playing the heavy, the CIA is revered by many liberals as a bulwark of integrity, its mission sacred, its conclusions unimpeachable. . . . The FBI draws similar adulation, never mind its history of spying on the likes of Ernest Hemingway, John Lennon and Martin Luther King.[21]

The US has also created domestic enemies, such as US peace movements that protested US wars in Vietnam, El Salvador or Iraq, or argued against US support of Israel in its brutal repression of Palestinians. During the Vietnam era, many Americans hated the Vietnam war, but hated the anti-war movement more, propagandized by the view that protesters were traitors. Today, we are told that Vietnam veterans defended their country and many of their "brothers" sacrificed their lives for the cause, even though Vietnam did absolutely nothing to the US. This is a reflection of the Security story that not only invents many of its own foreign enemies but also manufactures domestic enemies such as protestors against unjust US wars. Sociologist Jerry Lembke has written a book, *The Spitting Image*, based on extensive research showing that activists had not attacked or spit on returning veterans. In the *New York Times*, he talked about a reporter on the subject:

> The reporter was asking about accounts that soldiers returning from Vietnam had been spat on by antiwar activists. I had told her the stories were not true. I told her that, on the contrary, opponents of the war had actually tried to recruit returning veterans.

I told her about a 1971 Harris Poll survey that found that 99 percent of veterans said their reception from friends and family had
been friendly, and 94 percent said their reception from age-group
peers, the population most likely to have included the spitters, was
friendly.[22]

Lembke makes an important observation that the image of spitting
on has a long history in nations seeking a scapegoat for defeat:

> I pointed to the long history of spitting imagery in legends of
> betrayal. In the New Testament, Christ's followers spit on him
> in renunciation of their loyalty. Following Germany's defeat in
> World War I, soldiers returning from the front claimed to have
> been spat on by women and girls. The German stories were stud-
> ied by historians and found to be part of the "Dolchstosslegende,"
> or stab-in-the-back legend, that the military had been betrayed
> behind the lines, sold out at home.[23]

And Lembke's conclusion is compelling:

> Is the abiding American discomfort with the war it lost in Vietnam
> and the enduring allure of the spat-upon veteran stories indicative
> of betrayal preoccupations at work in our own culture? Is it the
> post-Vietnam lost-war narrative that feeds the back-to-the-future
> sentiments in campaign promises to restore and rebuild America?
> And are the recent public and political spectacles of nativism and
> gun-toting masculinity symptoms of a wounded people more than
> deviant personalities?[24]

The Security story treats all US wars as heroic defense against enemies,
a narrative that can only be debunked by a peace movement that res-
urrects itself and does not allow itself to be demonized as the enemy at
home. The weakness of the US peace movement is an agonizing sign of
how weak the Left has become in the US.

Beginning with the Reagan era, the residues of the left and peace
movement were bullied into not questioning the over-all purpose of

America's militaristic empire. At best they could say mistakes might have been made, but its ultimate intentions were always magnanimous. Sharing an underlying consensus with right wingers, dominant liberals, including both Clintons and Obama take it as a given, beyond discussion, that American interests must always triumph, that the US must always be hegemonic. You can debate specific details about tactics but you cannot challenge the underlying objectives. You must support the troops which means you must accept that the underlying purpose for which they are fighting and dying is noble. You need military credentials before you can challenge American policy. Cindy Sheehan was a gold star mother. Even Edward Snowden was an intelligence officer.

As in Vietnam, joining the military in Iraq and Afghanistan is being presented as noble heroic selfless service. This places the wars beyond the pale of moral condemnation, even among those who criticize it as a mistake. This attitude is held among liberals and some leftists, as well as conservatives.

Indeed, left liberal organizations like MoveOn, ActBlue and Progressive Turnout Project attack Donald Trump for his criticism of John McCain, Captain Humayun Khan-a Muslim killed in Iraq—and his parents. Although there is much to condemn about Donald Trump, his rhetorical opposition to nation-building and the Iraqi War are not among them.

Hillary Clinton had Khan's parents speak at the 2016 Democratic Convention to show Muslims can be "true Americans" who die admirably in American invasions of Muslim countries. As tragic as Himayun's loss may have been, nowhere in Khizr Khan's(his father) speech was there any indication of where the real blame should lie—on the war planners who sent him to die attempting to impose American interests on another country.

MoveOn wrote their supporters an e-mail asking for donations and demanding that Trump "show a Gold Star family the deference it deserves." In another e-mail requesting donations, ActBlue implied Trump is unfit for the presidency "after insulting American war heroes like Captain Khan." In an interview, Khizr indicated that late Republican

Senator John McCain, whom the North Vietnamese had imprisoned as a bomber pilot, was his son's hero.

With a few exceptions like Trump, both Republicans and Democrats uphold McCain as the epitome of self-sacrificing moral virtue, whom patriotic American children should grow up to emulate. McCain was captured after bombing villages, killing civilians, and destroying cities and infrastructure.

Progressives and the Left applaud McCain and Khan as heroes partly because they fear being branded by the Security story as domestic enemies. They dread being accused of hating America, undermining American capitalism and subverting American traditional values. That dread then is internalized, leading many Leftists to embrace US militarism in a subtle or disguised way without realizing how they are undermining their own core values.

We have seen that the Security story is entangled with the culture wars, and that US elites have mobilized Evangelical Christians and believers in "family values" to fight progressives as enemies of God and the nation, exactly the same manufacture of domestic enemies that fascist regimes did as they turned rural and small -town Germans against the traitorous urban secular "Jewish" German left. Yet that very Left could have protected all Germans against the horrors of perpetrating crimes against humanity and destroying the German nation. Instead Hitler successfully defined and destroyed the German Left as "the enemy."

There are lessons here for the progressives being defined as enemies of the mainstream Rust Belt workers or southern and rural whites. Progressives and the Left could help create the universal security—through political change in our capitalist and militarized system—that is in the interest of Republican Rust Belt workers and people of all races. But they have to tell that story in a way that the Rust Belt and "Red state" conservatives can hear, and in a way that respects them. Leftist sociologist Arlie Russell Hochschild, in her best-seller *Strangers In Their Own Land*, found a way to do that when she listened to their hurt and sense of disrespect from liberals. One of the people Hochschild got to know shared her basic feeling:

that (Rush) Limbaugh was defending her against insults she felt liberals were lobbing at her: "Oh, liberals think that Bible-believing Southerners are ignorant, backward, rednecks, losers. They think we're racist, sexist, homophobic, and maybe fat." Her grandfather had struggled as a desperately poor Arkansas sharecropper. She was a gifted singer, beloved by a large congregation, a graduate of a two-year Bible college, and a caring mother of two. In this moment, I began to recognize the power of blue-state catcalls taunting red state residents. Limbaugh was a firewall against liberal insults thrown at her and her ancestors, she felt. Was the right-wing media making them up to stoke hatred, I wondered, or were there enough blue-state insults to go around?[25]

Hochschild found that when she could surmount the "empathy wall," she could connect emotionally and politically with conservative and religious working Southerners. There is a lesson here for progressives in the culture wars, connecting to the "emotional" issues that surround all politics. Find common ground where you can, especially on the economy and environment, once you build trust.

Should reaching out in this manner sound "touchy-feely" or unrealistic, remember that Bernie Sanders, who explicitly fought for "democratic socialism," captured a lot of votes of religious people and Rust Belt workers that ended up voting for Trump. Such a progressive strategy does not mean capitulating to racism, sexism or jingoistic nationalism. But Sanders' vast electoral appeal across the country, and the fact that a Black president was elected for two terms, with majorities in many Rust Belt and mid-America states, shows that progressive politics can be organized in these areas. Indeed, as we write, we are already beginning to see the rise of a new progressive Left in the forms of successful teachers' and nurses' strikes in Arkansas, North Carolina, Oklahoma and other Red states. Progressives are beginning to embrace a style and policies—a new story for true security—that delivers safety and well-being to downstairs people on the other side of the culture war. Instead of domestic enemies, we would be seen as allies, but that will require other major changes discussed later.

Note first, though, the failing to call out the lies associated with invented or manufactured enemies has prevented the Left from the massive public education required to deal with the real threats we face. Most important are the existential threats of climate change and nuclear war that could end civilization. We hear very little discussion of these threats because the invented enemies headlined by the Security story suck up all the oxygen. People can only fear so many threats, so if invented enemies are not debunked, they will crowd out the emotional space necessary to contemplate the overwhelming existential ones.

As we enter the era of these double threats to human survival—climate change and nuclear war—it is a form of collective insanity that we are in denial about both of them. Trump ordered all federal officials never to use the term "climate change," and ended EPA investigation of it, as if denying it would eliminate the threat. Well, it hardly did that but it did wipe it off the minds of the millions in his base, who were focused on the manufactured enemies. The same was true of nuclear war; Trump argued that it was crazy to have nuclear weapons if we don't use them. This should be understood as a kind of genocidal narrative, a Security story that denies the largest security threats ever faced by humanity.

Obviously, any Security story that doesn't protect the human race from threats to its very survival is catastrophically sociopathic. But the liberals in the Democratic Party have been relatively quiet about climate change as well as about nuclear war threats. In fact, even the progressive leaders of the Democratic Party tend to worship at the shrine of national security and fail to challenge the enemies constantly being invented and fought. On the Left, the decline of the peace movement has also taken the threat of nuclear war out of the public mind, or left the subject to the hawks and Trumpists who actually increase prospects for nuclear war by rescinding agreements like the Iranian one and manufacturing endless enemies who can be fought with tactical battlefield nuclear weapons. Anti-climate progressive movements have been larger and more vocal. But activists but have not tied the climate crises enough to the immediate problems of economic and social security, arising from our capitalist house and the profits made off both fossil fuel and military spending. Interestingly enough, Pope Francis has, in his description of a weeping earth:

This sister now cries out to us because of the harm we have inflicted on her by our irresponsible use and abuse of the goods with which God has endowed her. We have come to see ourselves as her lords and masters, entitled to plunder her at will. The violence present in our hearts, wounded by sin, is also reflected in the symptoms of sickness evident in the soil, in the water, in the air and in all forms of life. This is why the earth herself, burdened and laid waste, is among the most abandoned and maltreated of our poor . . . More than fifty years ago, with the world teetering on the brink of nuclear crisis, Pope Saint John XXIII wrote an Encyclical which not only rejected war but offered a proposal for peace. . ., I will point to the intimate relationship between the poor and the fragility of the planet . . . we cannot adequately combat environmental degradation unless we attend to causes related to human and social degradation. In fact, the deterioration of the environment and of society affects the most vulnerable people on the planet: "Both everyday experience and scientific research show that the gravest effects of all attacks on the environment are suffered by the poorest".[26]

Until the public follows the money, in a mainstream conversation about capitalism and its priorities, it will be difficult to focus the public mind on climate change as enemy #1.

Failing the Emotional Test

Focusing and keeping public attention on one's story is essential to success in any political agenda. You have to have a strong message and it has to be crafted and presented in a way that resonates strongly to most citizens. That requires not just clarity and reason, but skill in tapping into emotions, since politics, like all of life, is driven heavily by emotions and the irrational side of the human mind.

Hitler made no bones about this. As seen in the last chapter, he believed that only a charismatic emotional appeal, laced with irrational propaganda, could attract a passionate following in the population. He was a master in playing to the emotions overwhelming the German people—including humiliation after World War I and fear about the severe economic crises in the peace that followed. He found emotionally compelling scapegoats and enemies, and attracted a fevered following based on the intensity of his emotional connection to the people.

Liberals and the Left, being far more committed to rationality and factual evidence, have been reluctant to play to emotions and the irrational. But politics is always emotional and humans bring strong irrational impulses to their politics. The Right has understood this far better than the Left—and their Security story resonates because it plays so effectively to fears and primitive instincts of survival, even as it misleads people about the real threats.

To build a story around true security, the Left should always use reason and evidence to persuade people, but must connect with people's basic feelings and instincts. Climate change is an important example, since it is the most dangerous threat to our collective security. George Monibot, a leading climate writer and activist, acknowledges the issue didn't become "real" to him until his daughter was born.

> One week before this book was meant to be finished my daughter was born. . . . Everything I had been thinking about became—for the first time—real for me.[27]

He continues that his daughter, then, really drove his activism:

> But this baby, this strange little creature, closer to the ecosystem than a fully grown human being, part pixie, part frong, part small furry animal, now sixteen days old, and curled up in my lap like a bean waiting to sprout, changes everything. I am no longer writing about what might happen to people in this country in thirty years' time. I am writing about her.[28]

Progressives should never stop presenting scientific evidence of climate change; the scientific consensus is so strong and dangerous that, when presented clearly, it arouses deep emotions related to survival. But because the impacts are long term and may not feel real to people, climate movements have to find way to reach the gut as well as the mind, or the Left will keep failing the "emotional test."

Since humans respond emotionally most strongly to immediate concerns which affect them personally, the climate movement has to find ways to make a long-term issue more immediate, even to people who are not feeling the effects now. One way is to present the climate issue in economic terms that are deeply personal and immediate, through what might be called "time-tricking."[29] People tune out climate dangers because they are long term and abstract. But you can make it a short-term emotional reality if you can connect climate solutions to your immediate needs, such as a better job or salary. Since any climate solution requires massive investment in green jobs and a clean infrastructure, the climate movement can represent itself partly as a movement for full employment and a better quality of life. Fossil fuel companies—oil, gas and mining—help run our current capitalist system and will never give up their short-term profits for longer term environmental benefits. But if people feel that their job prospects and wages, as well as quality of life, can immediately improve by investing in clean energy, the emotional impact of the climate issue will be personally transformative. This is why climate movements need to engage in time-tricking and start a personal conversation about capitalism, showing how capitalism drives climate change and how climate solutions can immediately help millions of working people get jobs and more economic security.[30]

Another way to start passing the emotional test is using sound tracks and visual imagery that touch the heart. When Trump went after asylum seekers crossing the border, he adopted the "zero tolerance" policy in 2018 that led thousands of young kids to be ripped away from their parents, as discussed in earlier chapters. Taking toddlers from their parents is intensely emotional for most people, but it took actual audio and visual tapes of the kids locked up in detention camps and crying for their mommy or daddy to make most Americans pay attention and begin organizing to stop the cruelty. Not until Americans heard kids sobbing and whimpering on audio tapes or saw a toddler girl weeping as she wanted her mother to stay with her did this become a story that touched the public. Immigration activists can make rational arguments about protecting asylum seekers but when they use emotional tools like the audio and video tapes at detention camps—or present emotive phrases such as "the Statue of Liberty is weeping"—they can emotionally move millions to action. In this case, it forced Trump to cave and keep immigrant families together in detention.

Failures of PC

The Right has expanded its ranks by its full-scale war on "political correctness" or PC. Why do so many people like Trump? One answer is that he says whatever he wants, and takes special pleasure in saying things that liberals and the Left hate to hear. Many Americans probably voted for Trump simply because he said "Merry Christmas" rather than "Happy Holidays." When he called out NFL superstars who kneeled during the National Anthem, demanding that they be fired if they didn't "respect the flag," he was playing to emotional sentiments of patriotism, and piling on by saying things that were not PC because the athletes were African-American. Meanwhile, as the media were featuring the terrible plight of the immigrant Central American kids taken from their parents at the border, Trump gave rallies with no apologies for the detentions, boasting of his "staying tough" in order to keep Americans safe from criminals crossing the border. This kind of "tough guy" talk got rave receptions from his base, a sign of how his followers love his naked contempt for the PC of liberals.

PC is generally seen as a kind of policing of language that prevents people from saying what they think. It reflects codes of speech that force politicians and ordinary people to publicly accept words and views that they hate. It enforces dogma and understandably creates rage because people feel their right to speak freely is being undercut in the name of tolerance, by PC that is a form of repressive intolerance.

On some campuses, if there is the slightest risk that course material might offend some students, professors are required to issue a "trigger-warning."

Oberlin College in Ohio already has gone further. . ., issuing official trigger-warning guidelines for professors that sound almost like a parody of political correctness: "Triggers are not only relevant to sexual misconduct but also to anything that might cause trauma. Be aware of racism, classism, sexism, heterosexism, cissexism, ableism and other issues of privilege and oppression. Realize that all forms of violence are traumatic."

Worse, the Oberlin guidelines go on to advise professors to remove "triggering material" from their courses entirely if it is not directly related to the course's learning goals. Such instructions come dangerously close to censorship. Chinua Achebe's novel "Things Fall Apart" is listed by Oberlin as one possible "trigger" book because of its themes of colonialism, racism, religious prejudice and more. At Rutgers, an op-ed in the student paper suggested that study of "The Great Gatsby" should require trigger warnings about violence and gore. And then what happens? Should students be excused from reading a work of great literature, or be allowed to read a sanitized version?[31]

PC is an emotionally fraught issue in the culture wars, and is widely seen as arrogant Leftist regulation of speech and culture. The Right relentlessly attacks PC as Left censorship imposed by liberal, educated elites. These include universities, Hollywood and the Democratic Party who shape the PC that makes the blood of conservatives and many ordinary Americans boil.

While Left PC is real, as we show shortly, the Right story is disingenuous because conservatives create some of the most controlling American PC. The Security story itself is a dominant form of PC. It makes us say to veterans "thank you for your service," even if you hate the wars they have fought in. It makes the failure to stand and say the Pledge of Allegiance a form of treason. It makes it anti-American to say that official enemies, whether Cuba, Venezuela or Iran, are not really enemies. It makes it impossible to say that any American war is "criminal" rather than a "mistake." It makes you un-American if you say America is trying to control the world for profit rather than help police it for good. It essentially says to protestors against American capitalism or militarism: "Love it or leave it!"

Nonetheless, the Right is rarely associated with PC. In the public mind, PC is a Leftist tactic seeking to shut down everyone else's right to speak. The failure to recognize Right PC is a sign of just how powerful it is. For when people don't think of certain values—such as patriotism or the nuclear family—as PC, it means the PC is so ingrained that is just seems like common sense and the only way to think. Nobody forces you to accept it because it seems so obviously correct—and there is no alternative that you feel is being suppressed.

But while we need to show over and over again how much PC is produced by the Right, this does not mean that we should ignore or discount Left PC. It is real and damaging. It is particularly pronounced when it comes to conversations about gender and race, but it can extend to many more areas. This is a serious problem for the Left, because its core value is to create freedom and encourage critical thinking.

The Right embraces dogma—such as fundamentalist religion—because it is consistent with its basic worldview. But the Left historically arose out of a rejection of authority, dogma and fundamentalism created by the religious authorities and ruling aristocracies of the Middle Ages. When the Left embraces purity of thinking—and imposes its own authoritarian dogma—it is undercutting its basic raison d'etre.

Every progressive and Leftist should pay serious attention to the long history of what we would now call Leftist PC. In Soviet, Chinese and other communist regimes defining themselves as Marxist or "Leftist," thought control became nearly as powerful as in Nazi Germany. This history should be sobering to any liberal or Leftist today. Too many states with Left ideologies have become authoritarian and dominated by rigidly defined state versions of Marxism, Maoism or other dogmas. These are garden varieties of PC that have poisoned many Left movements over a long period of time.

Today, attacking Left PC has become one of the Right's most powerful weapons because Left PC is real and resented by millions of ordinary people. It has become very difficult to talk about sex, for example, without parsing every thought and phrase. College students learn to tiptoe around any phrase that might be viewed as sexist. During the #MeToo

Movement, liberal actor Matt Damon suggested there might be a wide "spectrum of behavior" deserving different treatments:

> a difference between patting someone on the butt and rape or child molestation. Both of those behaviours need to be confronted and eradicated without question, but they shouldn't be conflated.[32]

Actress Minnie Driver responded with anger, telling Damon he had no place speaking about this issue, saying that men:

> simply cannot understand what abuse is like on a daily level. . . . I've realized that most men, good men, the men that I love, there is a cut-off in their ability to understand. They simply cannot understand what abuse is like on a daily level.[33]

Driver may have a point, but there is a need for talk here—and for empathy. By telling Damon he had no right to speak about women's sexual harassment, Driver was enforcing a kind of speech censorship that many see as PC. It violates the free speech principle that is at the heart of progressive and Left values, and it erodes belief in progressive dialogue and politics.

Likewise, universities have begun to enforce speech and behavior codes about dating and sexual behavior that turn the spontaneity of sex into a ritual of formally prescribed behavior that would seem to kill off healthy sexual impulses. Laws are being enacted like California Bill 967.

> California's State Senate recently passed legislation to target the crime on campuses. Bill 967, which passed unanimously and is also known as the "yes means yes" law, stipulates that colleges will receive state funding only if they adopt certain policies regarding sexual assault, chief among them being "an affirmative consent standard." For sexual activity to be lawful, "affirmative, conscious, and voluntary agreement" must be given. The bill goes on to assert that "Lack of protest or resistance does not mean consent, nor does silence mean consent. Affirmative consent must be ongoing throughout a sexual activity and can be revoked at any time."[34]

Such legislation arises from real issues about sexual consent, but there is danger that laws like this might violate one of the most fundamental principles of civil liberties, "innocent until proven guilty," as one feminist writes:

> In addition to creating a vaguely and subjectively defined offense of nonconsensual sex, the bill also explicitly places the burden of proof on the accused, who must demonstrate that he (or she) took "reasonable steps . . . to ascertain whether the complainant affirmatively consented." . . . "if both partners were enthusiastic about the sexual encounter, there will be no reason for anyone to report a rape later." But it's not always that simple. One of the partners could start feeling ambivalent about an encounter after the fact and reinterpret it as coerced—especially after repeatedly hearing the message that only a clear "yes" constitutes real consent. In essence, advocates of affirmative consent are admitting that they're not sure what constitutes a violation.[35]

Many influential feminists have begun to recognize these risks and have begun to critique this creeping dogma within feminist thinking. As with the Left generally, feminism arose to free sexuality and critical thinking rather than shut it down.

The same issues arise on race. Efforts to stop racism and racial violence in America are key aims of the Left. We must keep our eyes on the prize. But, as with sexism, the Left can verge into forms of speech control that shut down free and important conversations about race. In fact, honest conversations about both sex and race have become difficult in classrooms and political settings, for fear of saying things that might offend others who have "purer" ideas about what constitutes permissible speech. When conservative political scientist Charles Murray came to speak at Middlebury College, he was met with a massive demonstration.

> When leftists protest right-wing speakers on campus, they often deny that they are infringing upon free speech. Free speech, they insist, does not require their university to give a platform to people with offensive views. "This is not an issue of freedom of

speech," declared a letter signed by more than 450 Middlebury alums. "Why has such a person been granted a platform at Middlebury?" . . . Denying them that right—giving progressive students a veto over who conservative students can invite—comes perilously close to giving progressive students a veto over what conservative students can say. . . . In fact, Middlebury students did not only object to Murray because of The Bell Curve. Some also objected to his most recent book, Coming Apart, which analyzes the struggles of the white working class. (And about which Murray was scheduled to talk). Coming Apart, declared a group called White Students for Racial Justice, "uses largely anecdotal evidence to blame poor people in America for being poor, attempting to explain economic inequality through a perceived gap in virtue" and thus proves that Murray is "classist.". . . . As Murray approached the podium, dozens of students in the audience turned their backs, loudly read a prepared statement, and then began chanting "Hey, hey ho ho, Charles Murray has got to go," "Your message is hatred, we cannot tolerate it" "Charles Murray go away, Middlebury says no way" and finally, "Shut it down . . . ." If what at Middlebury, goes unchallenged, sooner or later, liberals will get shouted down too. To many on the campus left, after all, Zionism is a racist ideology. Drone attacks constitute war crimes. Barack Obama was the deporter-in-chief. Hillary Clinton supported a racist crime bill. Joe Biden disrespected Anita Hill. There will always be justifications.[36]

When the Left comes to be seen as shutting down speech, it is losing the battle for hearts and minds—and perhaps losing its own soul. This is not an argument to back off of creating new conversations and sensibilities to move us beyond racism and sexism. It's a virtue to challenge forcefully racist, sexist or classist arguments in campus discourse, including especially those made by famous invited speakers. But, unless it is hate speech, or speech encouraging violence, vigorously challenging or protesting the arguments is different than shutting down the speech and silencing anybody with different views than our own. It suggests the need to remember that free speech is the heart of all progressive and Left politics—and should never be subordinated to dogma in the name of justice or equality.

Of course, the Right is exploiting "free speech" in other ways. By equating money with political speech, in terrible decisions such as Citizens United, the Supreme Court permitted billionaires to contribute as much money as possible to buy elections, in the name of free speech. Likewise, advertisers get courts to strike down regulations on false claims as violations of their free speech. The Left needs to be clear that money is not speech and that corporate claims to "speech" are often specious. The Left thus needs to repudiate these abusive claims to speech, while being careful to protect freedom of authentic speech—whether on the Left or Right—as sacred.

To create a new society with true security, the Left and progressives have to be eternally reflective about whether it is cultivating its own dogma and cultivating its own PC. PC is one of the great emotional triggers of politics. One reason the Left has lost the "emotional test" to the Right is because Left PC is a serious real problem. The Left's ability to attract people at the emotional level requires eliminating as much PC as possible while ending racism, sexism and our system of militarized capitalism.

6

SAVING DEMOCRACY

HOW TO CREATE TRUE SECURITY

There's only one way out: for people directly harmed by the economic and political system to fight as one against the few who benefit from it.

—Rev. William J. Barber II

Politics hates a vacuum. If it isn't filled with hope, someone will fill it with fear.

—Naomi Klein

True security requires something entirely different than the Security stories we've described in this book. We need universal and true security for all people. Such a new story would address real rather than invented enemies. It would show how our militarized capitalist house needs to be transformed into a new democratic house of peace, stopping our billions going into war against endless enemies and investing instead in the social welfare and environment we need at home. It will enact universal human rights by universalizing resistance which

> brings all of our progressive movements and activists and our many unidentified and de-mobilized potential allies in the public—who make up millions of people—together in a common struggle against the system that threatens harm to everyone, and in favor of a new one that ends those universalizing harms.[1]

157

Real security requires leveling the upstairs/downstairs house, whose architecture is designed to create insecurity. The upstairs/downstairs house, our capitalist society, has insecurity built into its DNA—and can't function without it. As discussed in Chapter 1, the inequality and economic insecurity built into capitalism is not just a theory but a conclusion based on research studies of income and wealth distribution in 20 advanced capitalist societies over several centuries. Led by academic data-driven economists such as Thomas Piketty and Emmanuel Saez, research shows that capitalist economies are built to create and increase economic inequality over time, with the upstairs increasingly occupied by a "capitalist aristocracy" ruling on the basis of inherited wealth. There are few historical exceptions to this rule.[2]

This makes clear the irony of the capitalist Security story. *It promises security to the very downstairs working people that it forces into insecurity.* The house is built to divide and conquer, and to shift most of the wealth produced by downstairs workers to the 1% upstairs. The upstairs/downstairs house is an insecurity-promoting design that survives by obscuring the most important source of insecurity, that is, the architecture of the house itself.

This takes us back to the need for a progressive movement starting a new mainstream national conversation about capitalism and the insecurity promoted in a regime pursuing profits over people. Bernie Sanders showed that a mainstream conversation about "democratic socialism" is not a utopian project. Many European countries have long ago embraced versions of the "democratic socialism" that he championed. The EU has embraced the Charter of Fundamental Rights of the European Union—and constitutionalizes the universal human rights embodied in the 1948 UN Declaration of Human Rights:

> Much of the constitution is given over to the issue of fundamental human rights. . . . The rights outlined in the Charter of Fundamental Rights of the European Union go far beyond the rights contained in our own Bill of Rights and subsequent constitutional amendments. . . . If we were to sum up the gist of the document, it would be a commitment to respect human diversity, promote

inclusivity, champion human rights and the rights of nature, foster quality of life, pursue sustainable development, free the human spirit for deep play, build a perpetual peace and nature a global consciousness.[3]

Former French president Giscard d'Estaing proclaimed proudly that the document ensures that:

> Of all the men and women in the world, it is the citizens of Europe who will have the most extensive rights.[4]

European nations retain markets and other elements of capitalism, and they now face major tests of their universal human rights doctrines because they accepted hundreds of thousands of desperate immigrants, leading to Trump-style Far Right anti-immigrant parties. But despite the new European Right's rise, most European nations continue to pursue universal rights and to empower workers through the activism of a mobilized progressive population, strong unions and labor parties who provide job training, good jobs, wages, racial and sexual equality, education for critical thinking, for loving communities and universal rights—the basis of true security.

In discussing true security, we are focusing on deep institutional and cultural change that is not purely economic. People need material security to survive. But to flourish and develop all their human capacities, they need a much broader set of rights—including rights to health, education and fulfillment of individual creativity as well as solidarity in loving communities. We need to highlight at the outset that these broad forms of human fulfillment tend to be denied or limited in capitalist societies because they threaten power and profit. We start with universal rights as key to true security, because such universal rights are both impossible to realize in most capitalist systems and are the basis of material security as well as personal, community and spiritual fulfillment.

This expansive model of universal rights and true security is especially strong in Scandinavian countries—Sweden, Denmark and Norway—which linguist and political author George Lakey calls the nations of "Viking Economics."[5] They are also the models of Bernie

Sanders' "democratic socialism," and the agenda of progressive Democrats calling themselves "Justice Democrats." Known for their universal
social welfare rights—free college education, free universal health care,
generous child care and elder care programs, good public pensions and
Social Security, green environmental policies and inexpensive public
transportation, as well as purely defensive militaries and strong civic
communities that build trust and love, these societies provide much of
the true security that all humans need. This starts with basic rights and
universal access to all fundamental material and social needs—such as
jobs, education and health care.

When we ask our students whether this European Scandinavian
model appeals to them, they have questions but are envious of the
security it seems to offer. In one of Derber's classes, which included an
exchange student from Denmark, students had this discussion:

Danish student: *I go to the University of Copenhagen, the best univer-*
                         sity in Denmark.
American student: *How much is tuition there?*
Danish student: *I don't pay tuition. It's free.*
American student: *Hard to believe!*
Danish student: *It's even better. The government pays me to go to school.*
                         I get a stipend each semester.
American student: *I don't believe it. Is this because you won a special*
                         scholarship?
Danish student: *No, all students at the university get the same free tui-*
                         tion plus stipends to go to college.
American student: *And we are paying $70,000 a year to go to this univer-*
                         sity and are deep in debt.

When Derber asks students whether they would like to see the US
adopt this kind of system, the exchange in class goes like this:

Derber: *So what do you guys think of this? Is it a good idea for*
                         America?
American student: *How does the government pay for it? Somebody is foot-*
                         ing the bill?

Derber: *Taxes are high, because the government is paying for*
                           universal health care, child care, elder care and other
                           expensive programs.
American student: *How high are taxes?*
Derber: *They can go up to 60–65%.*
American student: *I still like the idea, but most Americans don't trust the*
                           government to do anything.
Derber: *True. Of course, Americans pay close to 45% in local,*
                           state and federal taxes—and feel they don't see much
                           return.
American student: *I think our generation might accept this—we liked*
                           Bernie Sanders when he proposed free public college
                           education.
Derber: *Yes, actually most millennials do support this—especially*
                           if they know that government spending is targeted specif-
                           ically to pay for free college and other popular programs.
American student: *This may be the fight of our generation!*

Our students are not alone. A majority of Americans, as documented
in the public opinion polls discussed earlier, support the universal social
welfare programs and worker rights enjoyed in Scandinavia. Moreover,
a majority of young millennial Americans now have a more positive
view of the word "socialism" than they do of "capitalism," a finding con-
firmed by multiple polling firms over the last decade, notably Pew and
Gallup. In one essay summarizing these attitudes:

> According to the conventional wisdom, the United States is a
> center-right country. But a new poll by Pew casts doubt on that
> idea. It shows widespread skepticism about capitalism and hints
> that support for socialist alternatives is emerging as a majoritarian
> force in America's new generation. . . .

> The story gets more interesting when you look at two vital sub-
> groups. One is young people, the "millennial generation" cur-
> rently between 18 and 30. In the Pew poll, just 43% of Americans
> under 30 describe "capitalism" as positive. Even more striking, the

same percentage, 43%, describes "socialism" as positive. In other words, the new generation is equally divided between capitalism and socialism. The Pew, Gallup and Rasmussen polls come to the same conclusion. Young people cannot be characterized as a capitalist generation. They are half capitalist and half socialist. Since the socialist leaning keeps rising among the young, it suggests—depending on how you interpret "socialism"—that we are moving toward an America that is either center-left or actually majoritarian socialist.[6]

This data is from 2010, but in recent years, the negative associations with capitalism and positive associations with socialism have steadily risen, particularly among Democrats and youth. Bernie Sanders, Keith Ellison, Barbara Lee, Elizabeth Warren, Nina Turner and other progressive leaders in the Democratic Party are responding to this new sensibility as well as helping shape it, but the views are bubbling up from the grass roots.

Many progressive activists are now fighting to restart a conversation about capitalism and institute deep reforms to create true security. The Rev. William Barber, a fiery North Carolina civil rights leader, has taken up the mantle of Martin Luther King to lead a "poor people's campaign" for system change. This comes from the heart—and his parents:

> I was born two days after the March on Washington [in 1963] to a family where my father was an activist and trained clergy. My father was one of the first science teachers to integrate a high school. My mother was the first black person to integrate the secretarial pool at the high school. So, in some ways, I was introduced to activism at an early age.[7]

Barber, who is emerging as the new Martin Luther King of our era, continues:

> Dr. King connected three issues: racism, poverty and militarism. He saw those issues as interrelated, bound together, that you couldn't address one without the other. He was very clear that in

order to address these interlocking injustices, you had to have an intersectional response. He said that the only hope for the nation moving forward was for all working-class and poor people to come together and form a powerful movement for moral justice—not just resistance—and that would hold these issues together and not separate them into silos.

Fifty years later and America has still not fully addressed these issues. Dr. King said in his speech following the Selma to Montgomery March that whenever there was the possibility of the black and white masses—especially the poor and working-class black and white masses—to come together, that they should.

This is why white aristocracy and others always sowed division and racism to prevent that from happening, because of how it could change the nation.[8]

Barber is really discussing a multi-racial "universalizing resistance" that he is putting into practice, drawing hundreds of thousands of supporters:

Dr. King never focused on just black people. That's the misnomer of the corporate and political reinterpretation of him. As early as 1958, he was talking about how the 1 percent was ruling over the 99 percent. The Poor People's Campaign had great diversity.

If you look down through history, change really only took place in this country when there were fusion movements. The abolitionist movement was black and white. The Reconstruction movement was black and white people. The only real hope for America is to have this kind of fusion coalition.

That's why we're visiting different communities from California to the Carolinas. We are going to visit homeless people, who are predominately white millennials, in Grays Harbor [County, Washington]. We will be on the Apache reservation [in Arizona] where multinational companies are trying to drill on sacred lands, which will poison aquifers, but the water won't stay on that reservation. It'll actually flow into the adjacent counties and towns, many of which are predominately white. When you look at all the states that denied Medicaid expansion, the majority of those people who got hurt were white—mostly in the South and in the Rust Belt.[9]

Barber is not the only activist thinking in these universalizing terms—and seeking system change through multi-racial movements. Many unions—especially the nation's biggest union of service workers, the SEIU, along with teachers' and nurses' unions—have taken to the streets in a new national multi-racial movement for economic security and justice. The unions are being awakened by a remarkable 2018 grassroots uprising of teachers, nurses and parents, especially in Red states.

We have seen wildcat teacher strikes in West Virginia, Oklahoma, Kentucky and Arizona. They are not fighting simply to increase their lousy pay, but for good schools and support for poor and working-class kids, all central to real security. In West Virginia, two teachers started organizing through Facebook:

> After O'Neal and Comer formed their Facebook group, membership quickly ballooned. By the end of January it had 20,000 members and had become a key organizing hub for teachers ahead of the strike.

> Teachers in the southern part of the state began holding local actions, staging "walk-ins" at their schools—handing out information to parents and teachers—and other areas quickly followed.

> "It was definitely bottom-up, not top-down," O'Neal said. The unions soon jumped on board, and the strike was born.[10]

Another group, called Red for Ed, started a similar teachers' movement in Arizona, co-founded by teacher Noah Karvelis:

> Red for Ed held a series of walk-ins at schools on 4 April, and more than 800 schools across the state will take part in walk-ins

on 11 April. Karvelis said they were inspired by teachers' success in West Virginia.

It's empowered everybody. It's shown us that you can do this, you can stand up, you can stand together and you can fight back and it's shown us that you can win.[11]

Five Reasons for Hope
Passing the Class Test

Five emerging conditions increase the prospect that a new fight for true security may be starting, even in the darkest ages of the Trump era. One is that the labor force is being demographically transformed, with the majority of workers now women and people of color. This means that identity and class politics will increasingly unite. Rev. Barber is just one of many African-American and civil rights leaders—including Rev. Al Sharpton, Nina Turner, Maxine Waters, and Barbara Lee—reasserting Martin Luther King's view that the civil rights struggle is inseparable from the struggle for economic justice and "democratic socialism."

More and more feminists agree, arguing that feminism is an economic justice movement. Many feminists didn't vote for Hillary but for Bernie Sanders and his "democratic socialism."

This is the direction that both socialists and feminists should be orienting themselves—toward struggles and demands that challenge both the drives of capital and the ingrained norms of sexism that are so deeply rooted under capitalism.

Struggles and demands that achieve this are concrete and are currently being fought for. For example, the struggle for single-payer healthcare—which would provide healthcare as a right to every person from cradle to grave regardless of their ability to pay—is a demand that undermines both sexism and the power of capital to control and repress worker agency. There are many other concrete short-term demands that blend the goals of feminism and socialism as well, including free higher education, free child care, and a universal basic income combined with a robust social safety net.[12]

Feminist leader, Susan Faludi, also calls for feminists to focus on broad changes for economic and social justice, saying:

> You can't change the world for women by simply inserting female faces at the top of an unchanged system of social and economic power.[13]

Even the National Organization for Women (NOW), the mainstream national feminist organization, is speaking out on economic justice:

> NOW advocates for wide range of economic justice issues affecting women, from the glass ceiling to the sticky floor of poverty. These include welfare reform, livable wages, job discrimination, pay equity, housing, social security and pension reform, and much more.[14]

Female and minority workers' most pressing needs include economic security and justice; these workers get paid less, they are the most impoverished, and they are becoming the majority of the workforce. So labor leaders will bring together fights against economic insecurity with fights for civil rights and women's rights. It is no surprise that unions of service workers, domestic workers, teachers and nurses are leading a battle for workers' rights and universal social welfare, since these unions are overwhelmingly female and people of color. The National Nurses United (NNU), the largest nurses' union in the country, has been on the front line in social justice protests and is aligning with the majority of women voters who know what pocketbook security means for them. The NNU embraces Viking economics as a measure of true security for women and for all workers, promoting universal rights:

•   *Win "healthcare justice, accessible, quality healthcare for all, as a human right."*[15]

As female-dominated unions and identity movements begin to challenge our economic system and fight for universal social welfare, we will get more of a real Left that can resurrect the mainstream conversation about capitalism that we urgently need to get to true security. We are seeing multi-racial and multi-gender progressive struggles not just to stop Trump but to build a new social order.

Indivisible: Building a United Front

A *second* hopeful sign is the growing integration of the Democratic Party with the Left and progressive movements on the streets. More Democratic congressional representatives and senators, pushed to the Left by the fierce anger of their base, have joined in many of the anti-Trump huge street protests, and even carried out sit-ins in Congress itself. Meanwhile, progressive organizations and social movements—led by groups such as Moveon.org, Indivisible, and Democratic Socialists of America—are increasingly working with elected officials and the Progressive caucus in the Democratic Party.

The Left collapsed in Weimar Germany because it could not unite the two leading Left parties—the Social Democrats and the Communists—nor did it integrate Left protest movements in German cities with electoral politics and the national Left parties. This breakdown of a Left "United Front" opened the door to Hitler. The corporatization of the Democratic Party since President Bill Clinton has created big divisions between progressive Left movements and the Democratic Party. But a new "United Front"—catalyzed by shared horror about Trump and unfettered corporate control of the country—is bringing together the Democratic Party with Left-leaning unions, Black Lives Matter, 350.org, immigrant rights groups, Moveon.org and feminist organizations. It is the only way to stop Trump and change the political power of both the corporate 1% and the Far Right.

Moveon.org is one model of Left organizing that brings together progressive activists—over 7 million of them across the country—to ally with and push the Democratic party toward true security. It seeks to support the most progressive Democrats, and push the entire Democratic Party. And they have had successes:

> Together, in collaboration with allies, we have grown the progressive movement and demonstrated that ordinary people's voices can

make a difference—that collectively, we possess extraordinary people power. MoveOn members have played crucial roles in persuading the Democratic Party to oppose and eventually end America's war in Iraq, in helping Democrats retake Congress in 2006 with our influential "Caught Red Handed" campaign, in securing the Democratic nomination for President Obama in 2008 with a pivotal endorsement before the Super Tuesday primaries, and in passing health care reform in 2010. More recently, we've surfaced student loans as a potent national issue, catalyzed the fight to expose and push back against the Republican War on Women, helped elevate the leadership of Senators Bernie Sanders and Elizabeth Warren and other progressives fighting economic inequality, mobilized more than half a million people to help take down the Confederate flag from the South Carolina state capitol grounds, led a massive grassroots mobilization to secure President Obama's diplomatic agreement with Iran and prevent a costly and unnecessary war of choice.[16]

Our Revolution, a grassroots Left movement growing out of Bernie Sanders' remarkable presidential primary race, is another example of how a United Front can be built. Sanders himself said about his campaign:

> Friends, this campaign is not just about Bernie Sanders. It is about creating a movement of millions of Americans. . . . in every community of our country. It is about fighting for a political revolution which transforms our country, and demands that government represents all of us, and not just a handful of billionaires.[17]

Our Revolution is seeking to make that revolution real. Nina Turner, former Congresswoman and the chair of Our Revolution, expresses the hope of a United Front:

> Our plan is to transform the Democratic Party; our plan is to run and elect progressive candidates; our plan is to make sure we continue to build local groups. Groups really are at the center of our universe.

We don't see everything from an electoral lens, as some organizations do. We see the bulk of our work through an organizing lens. That's the harder work, but we believe that if we can get people vested and engaged in the process, that over time sheer people power is going to force those who have the power to change.

It is a heavier lift, it's a longer lift. But let me give you a very real-world example. We can use Senator [Bernie] Sanders's Medicare-for-All bill. When he first introduced it, nobody would touch it with a ten-foot pole. But now, all of a sudden, he's got sixteen of his closest friends in the Senate standing by his side when he introduced that bill.

That didn't happen because people saw the light and said, "Oh yeah, Medicare for All is the thing." It happened because the American people are demanding that. That is why Our Revolution is committed to building these groups and giving voice to the people: because they are the force that will push the political class to where they need to be.[18]

The other hopeful development regarding United Fronts is movement activists running for Congress. In June 2018, a Democratic Socialist 28-year-old working-class Hispanic female, Alexandria Ocasio-Cortez, upset a top Democratic incumbent, Michael Crowley in New York City. She had been an organizer for Sanders and a Left movement activist on climate, immigration rights and a living wage. She is a firebrand progressive supporting a class-based politics for "democratic socialism":

Ocasio-Cortez characterizes narratives that pit race against class as a "fundamental misunderstanding" of how our country works: "I can't name a single issue with roots in race that doesn't have economic implications, and I cannot think of a single economic issue that doesn't have racial implications. The idea that we have to separate them out and choose one is a con."[19]

She is just one of many candidates from the activist Left who have taken the plunge into electoral politics, while staying activist in the streets. She ran as a "Justice Democrat," a national organization of insurgent progressive Democrats who are democratic socialists but call themselves "Justice Democrats" to win over all committed to social justice. She will be a leader of Left movements fighting to set an agenda for a far more progressive Democratic Party in Congress. After her victory over Crowley, she instantly became a national figure, an inspiring symbol of a new generation of activist Left progressives looking, like the Tea Party on the Right, to take over the Democratic Party and Congress. This may be the beginning of an all-out effort by Left activists to keep fighting on the ground while also seeking to enter and transform Congress. They want to keep working with their movement comrades in the streets and community organizing in an "inside-outside" alliance.

The failure to build a United Front has led to the virtual complete dominance of American government by the Republican Party and corporate America at this writing. The Tea Party helped create a Right-wing "united front" linking a fired-up Christian conservative base to a Far Right GOP now destroying the New Deal and creating an authoritarian plutocracy. The Left has to create its own Democratic Party for universal rights and democracy. If new efforts by progressives to grow and build a United Front grow and sustain themselves, they will catalyze a much more powerful political movement for true security. The challenge is huge, but essential and urgent.

Bottom Up

A *third* positive development is the growth and coordination of local and state progressive activists with national and global movements. Hundreds of cities such as Seattle, San Francisco, Austin, Cleveland and Boston are bypassing the federal Right-wing militarized state by creating their own true security agendas. They are raising local minimum wages in Seattle, creating sanctuary cities for immigrants in San Francisco, helping workers buy out their own companies and become worker-coops in Cleveland, passing their own climate and environmental rules as well as affordable housing and community economic development programs in Boston, investing in clean water programs in Detroit and Flint, supporting local social welfare and local infrastructure job programs in Philadelphia, rebuilding the entire social welfare system and infrastructure of San Juan and in rural Puerto Rico, destroyed in the 2018 hurricane, and rejecting the Right-wing federal programs that cut health care or send state National Guards to separate kids from their parents on the border.

Meet Kshama Sawant. She is the first socialist to win city-wide office in Seattle, and she is an economist who grew up in India. She belongs to Socialist Alternative, a political party organizing with local candidates in at least 20 major cities. She has successfully led the Seattle fight to enact the nation's first local $15 minimum wage—and is seen as the leader of the struggle for a new socialist agenda in Seattle.

> Sawant joined Socialist Alternative after hearing a speech from one of the group's members in 2009. Since then, she has worn her affiliation proudly: "People have an interest in rebuilding the left in the U.S.," she told me in an interview this week. "There are scores of young people who are looking for alternatives to capitalism."

> In keeping with the social justice themes of her campaign, she takes only $40,000 of her $117,000 a year council member salary and puts the rest into a self-administered "solidarity fund," which she uses to fund social justice campaigns. "This is not a question of charity," she told me. "You simply cannot be so far removed from the values of the people you're representing."[20]

Her activism is inspiring many local activists seeking economic justice in cities around the country.

> Sawant's advocacy is paying off—a $15 minimum wage plan with bipartisan support was proposed by Seattle's mayor earlier this month and will likely pass in some form later this year. Once considered unthinkably high, the $15 minimum wage is now being discussed all over the country—with everyone from striking fast-food workers to leading economists adding their support. Sawant has been credited as the driving force behind the movement.[21]

Another example of how to begin creating true security at the local level and then expand nationally is the worker-ownership or cooperative. Historian and economist Gar Alperovitz has been working for decades to build a cooperative economy of democratic socialism. He describes the momentum in Cleveland, where workers are taking over companies seeking to go abroad:

> In Cleveland's Glenville neighborhood—which is a poor, mostly black neighborhood with high unemployment and an average income of about $20,000—there exists a complex of worker-owned companies called the Evergreen Cooperatives.
>
> Evergreen is not a collection of small co-ops; these are significant scale companies linked together with a nonprofit community corporation, and they employ many local people. The largest urban greenhouse in the United States, Green City Growers Cooperative, is one of the companies in the complex, and it's capable of producing 3 million heads of lettuce a year, plus other greens. There's also Evergreen Cooperative Laundry, which is an industrial scale laundry serving hospitals and nursing homes in the area; they're housed in a LEED-certified building and use about a third of the heat and a third of the water of ordinary laundries. And there's a solar installation company, Evergreen Energy Solutions, which employs men and women from inner-city Cleveland and recently installed a forty-two-kilowatt solar unit on the roof of the Cleveland Clinic.[22]

Alperovitz sees this as building local alternatives that network together and create a sustainable model for national structural change:

> Taken together, these efforts are beginning to address one of the fundamental questions at the heart of our many crises, which is, who controls wealth?
>
> Throughout history, controlling wealth is a big part of controlling politics and, as a result, making decisions about the future. And

the richest four hundred people in America have more wealth than the bottom 180 million. So the efforts in cities like Cleveland to change patterns of wealth ownership at small and medium scales, local and regional scales, are very important in terms of building political power. They're doing it at the neighborhood scale, through cooperative forms, and within an ecologically intelligent context.[23]

This is how movements grow in America, from the ground up. The Right-wing big money monopoly over federal political power has got to be broken, but progressives are building local and regional movements uniting for systemic change in national protests and pressure on the Democratic Party. True security stories are being written at the local level but have to be rewritten and enforced at the national and global levels. Alperovitz is aiming to nationalize utilities and big banks to help build a new national cooperative and socialist system.

Winning Over Anti-Government Americans

A *fourth* positive development is the new sophistication of progressive groups that have figured out how to win support of Americans who don't trust "big government" or "tax hikes" for programs that claim to help them and are essential to real security. Most Americans describe themselves as against "big government" but they overwhelmingly support big government programs such as Social Security and Medicare, pillars of true security. The distrust of big government is strong and reflects the failure of the government to provide the security people need. But more progressives are finding that if they propose taxing the rich for very specific government programs such as free college or affordable health care, essential to true security, they can win real support.

A coalition in Massachusetts created a referendum on a tax on millionaires to pay explicitly for public education and public transportation:

> The Massachusetts Income Tax for Education and Transportation Initiative was certified for the ballot, but was then was blocked from the ballot by the Massachusetts Supreme Court on June 18, 2018, after the court ruled 5–2 that the petition should never have been

certified by the Massachusetts Attorney General, Maura Healey (D). The Supreme Court found that the initiative violated the state constitution, which prohibits ballot measures from mixing subjects that are not "related or mutually dependent." The measure would have created an additional 4 percent tax on the portion of incomes above $1 million for the purpose of providing funds for public education, roads and bridges, and public transportation. This tax would be in addition to the 5.1 percent flat tax currently in effect, for a total tax rate of 9.1 percent on income above $1 million.

Raise Up Massachusetts, the group supporting the Income Tax for Education and Transportation Initiative is still hoping to get their $15 per hour minimum wage initiative, and an initiative to establish a paid sick and family leave funded by a payroll tax on the ballot. Raise Up has been in negotiations with legislative and business leaders, retailers, and the Retail Association of Massachusetts to reach a compromise deal. Raise Up wrote in a press release regarding the court decision that they remain "strongly committed to winning a $15 minimum wage and paid family and medical leave for all Massachusetts workers this year, in the Legislature or on the ballot."[24]

The proposal won a lot of public support but was turned down by a court decision that quarreled with the breadth of the language. Nonetheless, the tactic of targeting taxes on the wealthy not just to go into the general government coffers but to be spent on specific programs offering true economic and social security is a brilliant movement strategy. Progressive movements in states around the country are pushing hard for tax-the-1% referenda; when spending is targeted for programs offering real security for millions of families, a progressive narrative in America can take root and create regime change at home. Yes, millions of Americans don't like taxes or trust big government in the abstract, but when taxes on billionaires and millionaires are levied to pay for very specific social needs, people go out and vote for them.

In the end, of course, we need national and global wealth taxes, as proposed by Thomas Piketty, to reinvest trillions in education, health, jobs and environmental protection and create true security across the nation and world. Piketty is famous for his proposal of a global tax on capital or wealth:

> if democracy is to regain control over the globalized financial capitalism of this century, it must also invent new tools. . . . The idea would be a progressive global tax on capital. . . . Such a tax would provide a way to avoid an endless inegalitarian spiral.[25]

Piketty is focusing on taxing wealth because it reigns in the new capital aristocracy; the tax helps equalize wealth but, ultimately is important because it is a step toward "democratic control of capital"—and thus central to sustaining democracy itself. He asks:

> How can sovereign citizens democratically decide how much of their resources they wish to devote to common goals, such as education, health, retirement, inequality reduction, employment sustainable development, and so on. Precisely what concrete form taxes take is therefore the crux of political conflict in society.[26]

Piketty has found another way to talk about what we are calling true security. Creating such security depends on democratic control over society's wealth, with ordinary people able to decide how much to spend on education, health, jobs and the environment to ensure their own security. He is not advocating putting government in control of all wealth but that the tax system must be administered through all sorts of local, state, federal and global governments, as well as non-profit and private channels to enforce universal rights and to fund them sufficiently to create true security.

While conservatives in the US are trying to eliminate the estate tax and other wealth taxes, a strong majority of Americans want to increase both income and wealth taxes on the 1%. They know that trillions of dollars—much of it squirreled away in "dark money" havens—are going to the rich. The only path to true security is to expose that wealth, make it transparent and gain control of enough of it through progressive taxes to guarantee security of jobs, income, health, education and other pillars of true security. Piketty points out that there is a long history of wealth taxes in nations such as France, the UK and other European states, who fund universal social welfare and thus have taken major steps to true security.

In the US, Sanders and other leading progressives favor "democratic control of capital" to win exactly the true security Piketty discusses. But, as in the Massachusetts Ballot, he recognizes that US distrust of government means wealth taxes should be targeted to funding essential social and environmental programs—such as his Medicare for all and free public college tuition—which are popular even among those who oppose "big government" precisely because they are targeted concrete programs providing true security. As more and more people are outraged by corporate tax concentration, 1% tax evasion and tax cuts on billionaires, a new revolution based on "no tax without representation"—led by ordinary people—may be growing.

The Millennial Awakening

A *fifth* positive is the growing progressivism of young people who are deeply insecure. College students are burdened with debt that can make it difficult to ever buy a house or save enough for retirement. Student debt in 2018 was about $1.2 trillion, even more than the total credit card debt Americans are carrying. The youth know the reigning Security story is not working for their generation. They are the first American generation who can expect to live less well than their parents.

Millennials are much more politically progressive than their parents or any other generation. More than 60% supported Bernie Sanders in the 2016 presidential campaign race. More than 80% voted for Sanders in New Hampshire, Iowa and other purple and red states as well as blue ones. They like his unabashed commitment to system change, which they think might be the only path to true security for them.

> The kids these days are doing fine . . . if you think socialism is fine. According to a recent YouGov poll, 43 percent of those ages 18 to 29 have a favorable view of socialism, compared with 23 percent of those over 65. Because only 26 percent of young people had an

unfavorable view (the rest had no preference), respondents under 30 were the only group more likely to report a positive view of socialism than a negative view.

But this isn't simply a youthful flirtation with supposedly radical views. Labels aside, there's something deeper going on: An analysis of national survey data reveals that on core issues of the role of government, young people are significantly more pro-government than their parents.[27]

The commitment to structural change comes out in their attitudes about issues most closely related to true security: guaranteed jobs and income:

Across different races, sexes, income levels and political affiliations, young people are significantly more supportive of guaranteed jobs and income than older people.[28]

And they are broadly supportive of government intervention on a broad range of true security issues requiring government:

Young people are more likely to agree that "we need a strong government to handle today's complex economic problems" (62 percent, compared with 55 percent of those 65 and older) rather than that "the free market can handle these problems without government being involved."

Similarly, when asked to choose between "the less the government the better" and "there are more things the government should be doing," the majority of those age 34 and younger say the government should be doing more, while nearly two-thirds of their older counterparts say that less government is better.[29]

This reflects an emerging new generation worldview in which students are seeing justice and true security in a "regime change" toward Scandinavian social democracy or democratic socialism:

For older Americans, socialism and capitalism evoke the Cold War animus between the United States and the Soviet Union. But data suggests that for young Americans, "capitalism" is a stand-in for the reckless system that created the financial crisis, while "socialism" brings to mind the social democracy practiced by Nordic countries.[30]

Change is almost always led by the young. Millennials are more likely to associate positively to the words "democratic socialism" than to "capitalism." There is no capitalist Security story working for them in the economy or in a violent society and world. The college students burdened by student debt understand the insecurity of their younger siblings in high school who don't feel safe there after Parkland and all the other mass shootings. They are viscerally afraid for their future and know the dangers of climate change and nuclear war.

A new American generation is feeling insecurity so deeply that it is hungry for a new national narrative and big change at home. Their fears can inhibit their activism; insecurity is paralyzing and they want to keep their nose to the grindstone for good jobs. But we are seeing thousands of spontaneous protests—from the Parkland students to Black Lives Matter to students blocking pipelines and calling for disinvestment in fossil fuel companies to ending costly never-ending wars, to strong calls for free college or relief of student debt. This may be a generation who will fight for true security because they know that the reigning Security story just escalates wars, economic austerity and their own personal debt and social insecurity, and violence in their own schools.

True Security—Local to Global

To fulfill the struggles for universal and true security, we need to move from a focus just on our house—or nation—to the neighborhood or global stage. There is no true and enduring security in one house without security in all of them. Without global or collective security, more power and security in one nation creates more fear and insecurity in another. That is part of why nationalism increases insecurity, and movement toward international solidarity is the only path toward true security. The Security story is so dangerous because it is a nationalist narrative that only increases the dangers of global catastrophe and shuts down meaningful conversation of true security for the world as a whole.

One obvious reason is that we live in a global capitalist system. All states are interconnected in the global financial community and the global corporations they support. When one house collapses, the others will run into deep crises themselves. This was obvious in the 2007 US housing mortgage and Wall Street meltdown which created a global crisis. US toxic financial instruments swept into banks from Iceland to Poland to Ireland to Japan and poisoned them. There is no security in one nation if a globalized financial system knits all economies together.

Second, the greatest enemies we face are climate change and nuclear war, period! Nothing can be achieved if we don't conquer these enemies because they will kill all of us. These are inherently global problems that cannot be solved by individual nations. If our greatest threats are global—created by a global order dominated by the US military and Western capitalism—there can be no true nationalist solution or security. It will take a change in the global order to make possible any real solution to the climate and nuclear war threats. This means any true security can only be achieved by global governance, with the UN and other collective security institutions, including international law and courts and development agreements that can bring all nations into common efforts such as the Paris Agreement on climate and the nuclear non-proliferation treaties.

Third, US nationalism—and the militarism that is at the very heart of all state-based nationalism—is the greatest threat to solving global crises and undermining true global security. American climate denial and Trump's trillion-dollar investment in the US nuclear arsenal, including for battlefield tactical nukes, are deal breakers for any true global security. The Security story is to protect the nation—and America's Security story says that it is seeking a peaceful world order as well as US Security. But it actually undermines the hope that the nation can survive by ripping up the foundations of world peace and collective security.

The US designed the UN to be weak and unable to contest American power, structuring it to be an instrument of the Western great powers in the Security Council. The biggest war in the world can be seen as between the US and the UN, a war that promotes US economic interests and protects global capitalism by weakening any international bodies that could create collective security and protect other nations against the US itself.

National security is the religion of nationalism but it intensifies insecurity by constantly manufacturing enemies. Nationalism is a recipe for endless war, the essence of US foreign policy since World War II. How can there be true security in a world defined by its most powerful nation as hostile and full of enemies trying to cheat it economically or weaken it militarily? And how can there be true security in a world where a superpower such as the US is predatory and violent, perpetually seeking profit and control over other nations who fear it as a leading enemy in their own national Security stories. A succession of Gallup polls shows that people almost everywhere in the world fear the US as the great threat to their own security and to world peace.

Building up the architecture of a global house—with world and regional as well as national and local government—is an absolute necessity for true security. This requires a global Security story, that doesn't eliminate the nation state but integrates it within a hierarchy of local-to-global governance and security institutions. The architecture of the global house should be based on the principle of subsidiarity, which does not mean concentrating all power in world government: quite the contrary. Rather, it argues that decisions should be pushed down to the lowest democratic level capable of ensuring rights and true security. Nation states need to move power up to international bodies to create climate and peace security but downward to localities to promote community and democracy.

> The state is an instrument to promote human dignity, protect human rights, and develop the common good. Subsidiarity holds that such functions of government should be performed at the lowest level possible, as long as they can be performed adequately. When they cannot, higher levels of government must intervene. This principle goes hand-in-hand with Participation, the principle

that all peoples have a right to participate in the economic, political and cultural life of society, and in the decisions that affect their community.[31]

Subsidiarity transfers much national state power and production to localities but also upward to regional and international bodies. In the end, as the UN Declaration of Human Rights makes clear, the universal rights that are essential to true security must apply to all people—or they will be available to none. In the Preamble, the Declaration makes clear universal rights means rights for every human on the planet, and has no relation to nationality:

> Now, Therefore THE GENERAL ASSEMBLY proclaims THIS UNIVERSAL DECLARATION OF HUMAN RIGHTS as a common standard of achievement for all peoples and all nations, to the end that every individual and every organ of society, keeping this Declaration constantly in mind, shall strive by teaching and education to promote respect for these rights and freedoms and by progressive measures, national and international, to secure their universal and effective recognition and observance, both among the peoples of Member States themselves and among the peoples of territories under their jurisdiction.[32]

Article 2 spells this out in black and white: universal rights and thus true security can only be created in a global society, applying to every human on earth:

> Everyone is entitled to all the rights and freedoms set forth in this Declaration, without distinction of any kind, such as race, colour, sex, language, religion, political or other opinion, national or social origin, property, birth or other status. Furthermore, no distinction shall be made on the basis of the political, jurisdictional or international status of the country or territory to which a person belongs, whether it be independent, trust, non-self-governing or under any other limitation of sovereignty.[33]

To create true security, we need to shift rapidly away from unfettered nationalism and its "national security" religion to the local-to-global paradigm. National security is a recipe for every-nation-as-enemy because it reflects and creates a Hobbesian world of sovereign entities who must fear that any erosion of their own power creates a power vacuum that other nations will move to fill. Global security creates global governance, international laws and courts, and global cultural open-ness that undermines the Hobbesian insecurity of sovereign and anarchistic nation states. This doesn't mean the end of the nation state but a realization that nations are simply one level of institutions concerned with global security—and that both global and local governance are essential to universal rights and true security.

Beyond the militarism that makes a nation-state world incompatible with true security and peace, we need to recognize that true security derives from the fulfillment of universal rights that only derive from a sense of solidarity and shared interests with all humans on the planet. Looking at the EU, where universal rights and security are most developed, Jeremy Rifkin notes that the various European Charters and Declarations of Human Rights have moved from national toward this new universal model:

> Citizenship is becoming increasingly international as human activity becomes increasingly global. The old idea of tying citizenship to nationality appears almost quaint in a world of global commerce, transnational civil society movements and shifting cultural diasporas.[34]

Rifkin goes on to say that the concept of universal rights—at the heart of true security—is independent of place and nation.

> Universal human rights eclipse any particular place. They exist independent of territory. That's why rights activists use the term "human rights" as opposed to citizen rights, to make clear the difference between the old idea of typing rights to territory and the new idea of de-territorializing rights and making them universal.[35]

Since true security requires fulfillment of universal rights, we need global movements and solidarity that are the foundation of international law and governance. Some sort of People's Parliament, based not just on representation by nations but by people's rising identity as humans inhabiting our fragile earth together, is central not only to solving climate change and nuclear war, but to put in place the democratic economic and political bodies that can tax global wealth and invest funds in education, health, jobs, the environment and all the other pillars of true security. This means uniting labor and other progressive movements worldwide for a global countervailing resistance to global corporations, which run the planet for themselves. One can universalize rights only by universalizing resistance for true security.

US elites seek a global economy for profit but embrace nationalism as a Security story because it is an emotionally riveting way to sustain capitalism itself. In a global world with open borders and extensive exchange between workers in other nations, the risk that the downstairs in each nation might unite with each other against the global capitalist order is a mortal threat to the capitalist system itself. It thus falls back on nationalism as a story about securing the nation, but it is actually creating more insecurity within its own house by manufacturing both foreign and domestic enemies that can't be allowed to go away and perpetuate a chronic sense of fear and insecurity.

The false security of nationalism—and the fact that national security inevitably and deliberately breeds endless enemies and deep insecurity—makes clear that true security is only likely to arise in a world based on cooperation, trust and international governing institutions. The only true security is now global. It is hardly surprising that the most powerful story of true security is global: the UN Declaration of Human Rights. The US has designed the UN to be sure that it can't implement these universal rights, but as global culture grows—and we realize how powerfully we all share the same human needs and rights—the political superstructure to achieve them will be built in the 21st century. If we fail, and stay wedded to nations and national security, we will never achieve true security and will most likely incinerate ourselves.

Universal and true security are what we all need—if only to save civilization and find personal well-being. We have no choice but to change our upstairs/downstairs house that generates endless insecurity. It's incredibly hard to do but if we don't try, we will doom ourselves and future generations to oblivion. We can do better!

NOTES

Chapter 1

1. Thomas Piketty, Thomas Piketty Quotes, Goodreads.com from Thomas Piketty, *Capital in the Twenty-First Century*. Cambridge, MA: Harvard University Press, 2014.
2. Ibid.
3. Peter Hooper, Matthew Luzzetti, Brett Ryan, Justin Weidner, Torsten Slok, et al. *US Income and Wealth Inequality, Deutsche Bank*, Jan. 2018 Deutsche Bank AG.
4. Ibid.
5. Ibid.
6. Ibid.
7. Thomas Piketty, *Capital in the Twenty-First Century*, p. 257.
8. Brenda Cronin, "Some 95% of 2009–2012 Income Gains Went to Wealthiest 1%," *Wall Street Journal*, Sep. 10, 2013, blogs.wsj.com.
9. *Blog for Social History of Television class at Virginia Tech*, Apr. 23, 2013, posted at blogs. it.vt.edu.
10. Sarah Lyall, "Rose, Fetch Her Ladyship a Sequel," *New York Times*, Apr. 1, 2011, nytimes. com.
11. James Walton, "How Upstairs Downstairs First Conquered the World," *The Telegraph*, June 22, 2018, telegraph.co.uk.
12. Ayn Rand, *The Fountainhead*, Speech by Howard Roark in Fountainhead Film, en. wikiquote.org.
13. Chuck Collins, *Born on Third Base*. White River Junction, VT: Chelsea Green Publishing, 2016, p. 21.
14. Ibid., p. 9.
15. "Poverty in the US," *Wikipedia*, en.wikipedia.org.
16. Alvin Gouldner, *The Future of Intellectuals and the Rise of the New Class*, New York: Palgrave, 1979.
17. Matthew Stewart, "The 9.9 Percent Is the New American Aristocracy," *The Atlantic*, June 2018, theatlantic.com.
18. Ibid.

19. "National Child Poverty Rate Remains Stubbornly High Despite Important Progress," *National Center for Children in Poverty*, Feb. 5, 2018, mailman.columbia.edu.

20. Antonio Gramsci, *The Prison Notebooks*, Slp edition. New York: Columbia University Press, Jan. 3, 2011.

21. Amy Sherman, "Did Donald Trump Inherit $100 Million? Politifact, Florida," Mar. 7, 2016, politifact.com.

22. Antonio Gramsci, *Prison Notebooks*.

23. Edward Herman and Noam Chomsky, *Manufacturing Consent*, Reprint edition. New York: Pantheon, Jan. 15, 2002.

24. Jeanne McGlinn, *Rags to Riches: The Horatio Alger Theme in Adolescent Novels About the Immigrant Experience*. Blacksburg, VA: Virginia Tech, University Libraries, scholar.lib. vt.edu. see also Horatio Alger, *Ragged Dick*. CreateSpace, Oct. 2, 2009.

25. "Rags to Riches," *Wikipedia*, en.wikipedia.org.

26. Ibid.

27. Ibid.

28. Charles Derber, *The Wilding of America*, 6th edition. New York: Worth Publishers, 2014.

29. Thomas Piketty, *Capitalist in the Twenty-First Century*, pp. 416–417.

30. Ayn Rand, *Howard Roark's Address to the Jury, The Fountainhead*, American Rhetoric: Movie Speech, 1949, americanrhetoric.com.

31. Ayn Rand, *The Fountainhead*. NAL, Centennial edition, Apr. 26, 2005.

32. Max Weber, *The Protestant Ethic and the Spirit of Capitalism*, 1st edition. New York: Routledge, May 25, 2001.

33. See Chapters 3 and 4 of this book, where we flesh out the role of the intellectuals and PMC in capitalist culture wars.

34. Chuck Collins, *Born on Third Base*, pp. 32–3.

35. Malcolm Gladwell, cited in Collins, p. 43.

36. Chuck Collins, *Born on Third Base*.

37. Ibid., pp. 59–60.

38. Ayn Rand, *The Fountainhead*.

39. Matthew Stewart, "The Birth of a New Aristocracy," *The Atlantic*.

40. Thomas Piketty, cited in Charles Derber, *The Disinherited Majority: Thomas Piketty and Beyond*. New York: Routledge, 2015, p. 58.

41. Matthew Stewart, "The Birth of a New Aristocracy."

42. Ibid.

43. "CEO Pay: How Much Do CEOs Make Compared to Their Employees?" payscale.com.

44. Keith Ellison, "New Report Exposes Extreme Inequality Between CEO and Worker Pay," May 16, 2018, ellison.house.gov.

45. Edward Hilmore, "'CEOs Don't Want This Released': US Study Lays Bare Extreme Pay-Ratio Problem," *The Guardian*, May 16, 2018, theguardian.com.

46. "Consumers Care about CEO Pay Ratios," *WSJ*, Mar. 12, 2018, www.wsj.com/articles/consumers-care-about-ceo-employee-pay-ratios-1526868301.

47. Thomas Piketty, *Capital in the Twenty-First Century*, p. 332.

48. Charles Derber and Yale R. Magrass, *Capitalism: Should You Buy It?* New York: Routledge, 2016, Chapter 6.

49. Thomas Piketty, *Capital in the Twenty-First Century*, pp. 358–359.

50. Thomas Piketty, Ibid., p. 351. See also Charles Derber, *The Disinherited Majority*, Introduction.

51. Ibid., p. 428.

52. Ibid., p. 26.

Chapter 2

1. Telegraph Reporters; London, UK; Sep. 10, 2016.
2. Tim Reid, "'Joe the Plumber' Praises Trump, cites his 'Beautiful Women'," *Reuters*, Mar. 4, 2016.
3. Ibid.
4. Nicki Swift, *Whatever Happened to Joe the Plumber*, www.nickiswift.com/75961/whatever-happened-joe-plumber/?utm_campaign=clip.
5. Jeremy Peters, "As Critics Assail Trump, His Supporters Dig in Deeper," *New York Times*, June 23, 2018, nytimes.com.
6. George Orwell, 1984, New York: Signet Classics, 1950. Part 3, Chapter 4.
7. Ibid., pp. 11, 14–15.
8. Noam Chomsky, cited in Charles Derber, *Marx's Ghost*. New York: Routledge, 2011, p. 90.
9. Noam Chomsky, *The Essential Chomsky*. New York: New Press, 2008.
10. Eric Fromm, *Escape from Freedom*. New York: Holt, Rinehart and Winston, 1968, p. 4.
11. Karl Mannheim, *Democratization of Culture* (first published in German, 1933). New York: Oxford University Press, 1956, p. 456.
12. Romans, *Revised Standard Version*. Oxford, U.K.: Oxford University Press, Chapter 13, V1.
13. From Karl Mannheim (edited by Kurt Wolff), New Brunswick, NJ: Transaction Press, 2011. See also, *The Great Chain of Being*. CUNY, n.d. Web. Aug. 31, 2015, http://faculty.up.edu/asarnow/greatchainofbeing.htm.
14. Ibid.
15. Barack Obama, cited in Ed Pilkington, "Obama Angers Midwest Voters with Guns and Religion Remark," *The Guardian*, Apr. 14, 2008, theguardian.com.
16. Amy Chozick, "Hillary Clinton Calls Many Trump Backers 'Deplorables', and GOP Pounces," *New York Times*, Sep. 10, 2016, nytimes.com.
17. Thomas Piketty, *Capital in the Twenty-First Century*, Introduction.
18. Marc Bloch, *Feudal Society*. Chicago: University of Chicago Press, 1961, p. 241.
19. Ibid., p. 241.
20. Ibid., p. 265.
21. Erich Fromm, *Escape from Freedom*, p. 34.
22. Marc Bloch, *Feudal Society*, p. 145.
23. Ibid., p. 146.
24. Ibid., p. 145.
25. Ibid., p. 146.
26. Donald Trump, Acceptance Speech to Republican National Convention, cited in Yoni Appelbaum, "I Alone Can Fix It," *The Atlantic*, July 21, 2016, theatlantic.com.
27. Charles Derber, *The Disinherited Majority*, Chapter 5.
28. Ibid. See also Thomas Piketty, *Capital in the Twenty-First Century*, Introduction.
29. From Karl Mannheim, originally published in Karl Mannheim, *Conservative Thought*. New York: Oxford University Press, 1953, p. 292.
30. Ibid., p. 456.
31. Marc Bloch, *Feudal Society*, p. 148.
32. Ibid., p. 149.
33. Ibid., p. 73.
34. Ibid., p. 85.
35. Ibid., p. 83.

Chapter 3

1. Donald Trump, cited in Brad Plumer, "Full Transcript of Donald Trump's Acceptance Speech at the RNC," July 22, 2016, Vox.com.
2. Ibid.
3. Julie Hirschfeld Davis and Niraj Chokshi, "Trump Defends 'Animals' Remark, Saying It Referred to MS-13 Gang," *New York Times*, May 17, 2108, nytimes.com.
4. Donald Trump, *The Inaugural Address*, Jan. 20, 2017, whitehouse.gov.
5. Donald Trump, Acceptance Speech, Republican National Convention, July 2016.
6. Donald Trump, *Trump Supporters Assault Black Protesters: Maybe He Deserved to be Roughed Up.* Reverb Press, Nov. 23, 2015, reverbpress.com.
7. Michael Finnegan and Noah Birman, "Trump's Endorsement of Violence Reaches New Level: He May Pay Legal Fees for Assault Suspect," *LA Times*, Mar. 13, 2016, latimes.com.
8. Donald Trump, Closing political argument, Nov. 4, 2016.
9. Thomas Frank, "Millions of Ordinary Americans Support Donald Trump. Here's Why," *The Guardian*, Mar. 7, 2016, theguardian.com.
10. Ibid.
11. Ibid.
12. Donald Trump, cited in Chris Cillizza, *Donald Trump Thinks Not Clapping for Him Is Treasonous.* CNN, Feb. 6, 2018, cnn.com.
13. Lauren Markoe, "Did God Choose Trump? What It Means to Believe in Divine Intervention," *Religious News Service*, 2018, cnn.com.
14. Donald Trump, Immigration rally, Aug. 22, 2016, Akron, Ohio.
15. Donald Trump, cited in Robert Windrew and William Arkin, "What Does Donald Trump Really Think About Using Nuclear Weapons?" *NBCNews*, Sep. 28, 2016, Nbcnews.com.
16. Donald Trump, *Inaugural Address*, Jan. 20, 2017, whitehouse.gov.
17. Ibid.
18. Ibid.
19. Ibid.
20. Donald Trump, *2016 RNC Draft Speech Transcript.* Arlington, VA: Politico, July 21, 2016.
21. Charles Derber and Yale R. Magrass, *Morality Wars.* New York: Routledge, 2010.
22. George Orwell, *1984.*
23. Donald Trump, cited in Miriam Valverde, "Immigration, MS-13 and Crime: The Facts and Donald Trump's Exaggerations." Politifact, Feb. 7, 2018.
24. John Wagner, "Trump Says He Has 'Absolute Right' to Pardon Himself of Federal Crimes but Denies any Wrongdoing," Washington Post; June 4, 2018.
25. Rudy Giuliani, cited in Veronica Stracqualursi and Dana Bash, *Giuliani to Huffpost: Trump Could Have 'Shot' James Comey' and Not Be Prosecuted.* CNN, June 4, 2018, cnn.com.
26. Ibid.
27. Richard Nixon, cited in "Context of April 6, 1977: Nixon: 'If the President Does it, That Means it's Not Illegal,'" Interview with David Frost. historycommon.org.
28. Max Book, *Wall Street Journal*, July 15, 2003, zeroanthropology.net.
29. Rudyard Kipling, "The White Man's Burden": Kipling's Hun to US Imperialism, Feb. 1899, historymatters.gmu.edu. See also Rudyard Kipling, *"The White Man's Burden: The United States & The Philippine Islands, 1899." Rudyard Kipling's Verse: Definitive Edition.* Garden City, New York: Doubleday, 1929.

30. David Vine, "The Military's New Lily-Pad Strategy," *The Nation*, July 16, 2012, thenation.com.
31. Barack Obama, cited in "Islamic State Crisis: Key Quotes from Obama," *BBC News*, Sep. 11, 2014, bbc.com.
32. Fred Fleitz, cited in Peter Beinart, "A Radical Pick for the National Security Council," *The Atlantic*, June 1, 2018, theatlantic.com.
33. Gabriella Paielta, "UN Condemns US Practice of Separating Migrant Children from Parents," *The Cut*, June 5, 2018, thecut.com.
34. Donald Trump, cited by Lisa W. Foderaro, "Angered by Attack, Trump Urges Return of the Death Penalty," ads published in four *New York City* Newspapers, 1989, nytimes.com.
35. Charles Derber, *The Wilding of America*, 6th edition. New York: Worth Publishers, 2014.
36. Donald Trump, "Central Park Five Settlement is a Disgrace," *New York Daily News*, 1989, nydailynews.com.
37. Donald Trump, tweet @RealDonaldTrump, June 14, 2018.
38. Charles Blow, "A Rebel, A Warrior and a Race Fiend," *New York Times*, Sep. 25, 2017, nytimes.com.
39. Donald Trump, cited in Charles Blow, ibid.
40. Rich Lowry, "Trump's New Culture War Has Left Liberals Reeling. They Thought They'd Won that Battle," *The Guardian*, Jan. 29, 2017, theguardian.com.
41. Ibid.
42. Bernie Sanders, "Bernie Sanders Quotes," BrainyQuote, brainyquote.com.
43. Tim Reid, "'Joe the Plumber' Praises Trump, cites His 'Beautiful Women'," *Reuters*, Mar. 4, 2016.
44. Ibid.
45. Nicki Swift, *Whatever Happened to Joe the Plumber*, www.nickiswift.com/75961/whatever-happened-joe-plumber/?utm_campaign=clip.
46. Charles Derber, *Wilding of America*. New York: Worth, 2014, Chapter 1.
47. Charles Derber and Yale R. Magrass, *Bully Nation*. Lawrence, KS: University Press of Kansas, 2017, p. 10.
48. Summary of discussions and reports from students in Derber's classes in Spring, 2018.
49. Editorial, "Chinese Tariffs Are Already Hitting Trump Voters," *New York Times*, June 15, 2018, nytimes.com.
50. Bobby Cervantes, *Ten Top Quotes from the NRA's La Pierre*. Politico, Dec. 21, 2012, politico.com.
51. Ibid.
52. "'The Top Ten Guns Women Buy,' The Well Armed Woman: Where the Feminine and Firearms Meet," https://thewellarmedwoman.com/about-guns/the-top-10-guns-women-buy/.
53. Charles Derber and Yale R. Magrass, *Bully Nation*.
54. Ayn Rand, *The Virtue of Selfishness*. New York: Signet Paperback Edition, 1954.
55. Charles Derber, *The Wilding of America*.

Chapter 4

1. Sean Gallagher, "NY Times Reporter's Emails Seized by Justice Dept. in Senate Intel Committee Leak Case," ARS Technica, *arstechnica*.com, June 8, 2018.
2. Michael M. Grynbaum, "Press Groups Criticize the Seizing of a *Times* Reporter's Records," *New York Times*, June 8, 2018, nytimes.com.

3. Brian Tashman, "Donald Trump Thinks the Freedom of the Press is Disgusting". ACLU, ACLU.org, Oct. 13, 2017.
4. *New York Times*, June 14, 2018, nytimes.com.
5. Madeline Albright, *Fascism: A Warning*. New York: Harper, Apr. 2018.
6. Steven Levitsky and Daniel Ziblatt. *How Democracies Die*. New York: Crown, Jan. 2018.
7. Timothy Snyder, *On Tyranny*. New York: Tim Duggan Books, Feb. 2017.
8. Timothy Snyder, *The Road to Unfreedom*. New York: Tim Duggan Books, Apr. 2018.
9. Bertram Gross, *Friendly Fascism*. Boston: South End Press, 1999.
10. Philip Roth, *The Plot Against America*. New York: Vintage, 2005.
11. Sinclair Lewis, *It Can't Happen Here*. New York: Signet Classics, 2005.
12. Timothy Snyder, *On Tyranny*. Cited in *On Tyranny*, GoodReads Quotes.
13. Ibid.
14. Ibid.
15. Charles Derber and Yale R. Magrass, *Morality Wars*, Chapter 4, p. 84.
16. Mussolini, cited in ibid., p. 84.
17. Ibid., pp. 84–85.
18. Adolph Hitler, *Mein Kampf*, Reprint edition. New York: Elite Minds Inc., Apr. 14, 2009.
19. Adolph Hitler; Speech Before the Reichstag Declaring War Against the United States; Dec 11, 1941; As recorded by the Monitoring Service of the British Broadcasting Corporation. www.sunsite.unc.edu/pha/policy/index.html Words of Peace-Words of War; Jewish Virtual Library; www.jewishvirtuallibrary.org/hitler-s-speech-declaring-war-against-the-united-states.
20. Adolph Hitler, *Mein Kampf*. Free Thought Books, Mar. 23, 2016. First edition in GermanFranz Eher Verlag, July 18, 1925, p. 131. cited on nationalists.org.
21. Ibid., p. 134.
22. Ibid., p. 40.
23. Adolph Hitler, cited in "Adolph Hitler," Wikiquote, en.wikiquote.org.
24. Adolph Hitler, cited in *Adolf Hitler on God: Quotes Expressing Belief and Faith*, ThoughtCo, www.thoughtco.com.
25. Adolph Hitler, *Mein Kampf*. New York: Free Thought Books, 2016, p. 161, also cited on AZ Quotes azquotes.com.
26. Adolph Hitler, *Mein Kampf*, cited on nationalists.org, p. 41.
27. Adolph Hitler, Speech of Apr. 12, 1922, Quoted in Hitler, My New Order.
28. Timothy Snyder, *On Tyranny*, cited in *On Tyranny* Goodreads Quotes, goodreads.com/ quotes.
29. Adolph Hitler, cited in Adolph Hitler, AZ Quotes, azquotes.com.
30. Adolph Hitler, *Mein Kampf*, cited on Adolph Hitler quotes, nationalists.org.
31. Adolph Hitler, "Adolph Hitler Quotes," BrainyQuote, brainyquote.com.
32. Adolph Hitler, *Mein Kampf*, cited on *Mein Kampf*, Wikiquote, en.wikiquote.org.
33. Adolph Hitler, cited in "Adolph Hitler Quotes," BrainyQuote, brainyquote.com.
34. Ibid.
35. John Maynard Keynes, *The Economic Consequences of the Peace*. Chicago: Rogers Fischer Publishing, 2013.
36. Adolph Hitler, "Hitler Quotes," Jan. 30, 1941, nationalists.org.
37. Adolph Hitler, "Hitler Quotes," nationalists.org.
38. Adolph Hitler, "Telegram to FDR," 1938.
39. Adolph Hitler, *Mein Kampf*. Free Thought Books, p. 131, cited also on "Hitler Quotes," nationalists.org.
40. Adolph Hitler, *Mein Kampf*, p. 253, cited also on "Hitler Quotes," nationalists.org.
41. Ibid., p. 56 cited also on "Hitler Quotes," nationalists.org.
42. Ibid., p. 356 cited also on "Hitler Quotes," nationalists.org

43. Ibid., p. 360. cited also on "Hitler Quotes," nationalists.org.
44. Yoni Appelbaum, "I alone can fix it," *The Atlantic*, July 24, 2016, www.theatlantic.com/politics/archive/2016/07/trump-rnc-speech-alone-fix.
45. Philip Rucker, "'Dictator envy': Trump's Praise of Kim Jong Un Widens His Embrace of Totalitarian Leaders," *Washington Post*, June 15, 2018 posted on *The Washington Post* (WP Company LLC).
46. Cited in David M. Kennedy, *Over Here: The First World War and American Society*. New York: Oxford University Press, 2004. ISBN 0-19-517399-6.
47. Charlie Savage, *Takeover*, Reprint edition. Boston: Back Bay Books, Apr. 28, 2008.
48. Charlie Savage, *Power Wars*, Revised edition. Boston: Back Bay Books, June 27, 2017.
49. Charlie Savage, Quoted in PBS Interview with Charlie Savage, www.pbs.org/wgbh/pages/frontline/cheney/themes/statements.html.
50. Ibid.
51. *Goodreads Book Overview of Power Wars*, www.goodreads.com/topic/show/19038627-d0wnload-power-wars-pdf-audiobook-by-charlie-savage.
52. Louis Brandeis, cited in www.brandeis.edu/legacyfund/bio.html.
53. Bernie Sanders, quoted in "Bernie Quotes for a Better World," betterworld.net.
54. Bernie Sanders, quoted in ibid.
55. Rand Paul, cited in Rand Paul Quotes brainyquote.com, see also www.brainyquote.com/quotes/rand_paul_704498.
56. For documentation of scores of such stories, see Charles Derber, *The Wilding of America*, 6th edition. New York: Worth Publishers, 2014.
57. David Hemenway, *Private Guns, Public Health*. Ann Arbor, MI: University of Michigan Press, 2013.
58. Cheney cited in "Biden vs. Cheney: Battle of the Vice Presidents". "On the Record" with Greta Van Susteren, www.foxnews.com, Feb. 16, 2010. See also "Dick Cheney Quotes About Terrorism," azquotes.com.
59. Lauren Gambino, "Trump Repeats Call to Deport Undocumented Migrants Without Due Process," *The Guardian*, June 25, 2018, theguardian.com.
60. Trump, cited in Gambino, *The Guardian*, ibid.
61. Samuel Huntington, *Clash of Civilizations and the Remaking of the World Order*. New York: Simon & Schuster, 2011.
62. Richard Spencer, Interview with Time Magazine, Apr. 2016 cited also in Kasia Kovacs, "'Richard Spencer Quotes' 12 Things White Nationalist Leader of Alt-Right Movement Has Said About Race, Immigration and Trump," *International Business Times*, Feb. 25, 2017, ibtimes.com.
63. Richard Spencer, Speech at Texas A&M, Dec. 2016 cited also in Kasia Kovacs, ibid.
64. Richard Spencer, cited in Kasia Kovacs, ibid.
65. Ibid.
66. BuzzFlash, Is the Republican Party Still the Racist, Character-Assassination, Culture Wars' Squad Created by Lee Atwater? Ask Stefan Forbes, Jan. 27, 2009, buzzflash.com.

Chapter 5

1. See Charles Derber, *Welcome to the Revolution: Universalizing Resistance in Perilous Times*. New York: Routledge, 2017.
2. Robert F. Kennedy, "RFK's Ripple of Hope Speech in South Africa," cited on NPR, June 30, 2013, National Public Radio, Inc.
3. Mark Twain, Mark Twain Quotes. BrainyQuote, brainyquote.com.

4. Donald Trump, cited in Rosie Gray, "Trump Defends White-Nationalist Protesters: 'Some Very Fine People on Both Sides,'" *The Atlantic*, Aug. 15, 2017, theatlantic.com.

5. See Charles Derber, *Regime Change Begins at Home*. San Francisco: Berrett-Koehler Publishers, 2004. See also Derber, *Corporation Nation*. New York: St. Martin's Press, 2000.

6. Charles Derber, *Hidden Power*. San Francisco: Berrett-Koehler Publishers, 2005.

7. Donald Trump, tweet at @realDonaldTrump, June 19, 2018.

8. Peter Dreier, "Most Americans are Liberal, Even if They Don't Know It," *The American Prospect*, Nov. 10, 2017, Prospect.org.

9. Paul Hawken, *Blessed Unrest*. New York: Penguin, 2008.

10. Eugene Debs, Speech in Canton Ohio, June 16, 1918.

11. Martin Luther King, Speech to Southern Christian Leadership Conference (SCLC) board on Mar. 30, 1967.

12. Martin Luther King, Speech to SCLC, Aug. 16, 1967.

13. The Simpsons, www.reddit.com/r/ShitLiberalsSay/comments/8309uj/an_outrage/ March 8, 2018.

14. Cited in NTanya Lee and Steve Williams, "More than We Imagined: Activists' Assessments on the Moment and the Way Forward," Ear to the Ground report, May 2013, http://eartothegroundproject.org.

15. Shifra Freewoman, *Why Lesbians and Gays Should Be Banned from the Military*. Boston: Spare Change News, Nov. 6–Nov. 18, 2008.

16. Martin Luther King, Speech to SCLC, Aug. 16, 1967.

17. Norman Solomon, "Is MSNBC Now the Most Dangerous Warmonger Network?" *Truthdig*, Mar. 1, 2018, truthdig.com.

18. Robert Parry, cited in Norman Solomon, ibid.

19. Noam Chomsky, "Noam Chomsky on How the Iraq War Birthed ISIS and Why US Policy Undermines the Fight Against it," *Democracy Now*, Mar. 2, 2015, democracynow.org.

20. Matt Sledge, "Every Yemen Drone Strike Creates 40 to 60 New Enemies, Former US Official Says," *Huffington Post*, Oct. 23, 2013, huffpost.com.

21. Walter Kerr, *Illiberal Value*. New York: Harpers, Aug. 2018, p. 7.

22. Jerry Lembke, "The Myth of the Spitting Antiwar Protester," *New York Times*, Oct. 13, 2017, nytimes.com.

23. Ibid.

24. Ibid.

25. Arlie Russell Hochschild, *Strangers in Their Own Land*. Quote cited in "Arlie Russell Hochschild quotes," goodreads.com.

26. Pope Francis, *Encyclical Letter Laudato Si' of the Holy Father Francis on Care for Our Common Home Vatican*. Rome Italy: The Holy See, May 2015.

27. George Monibot, *Heat: How to Stop the Planet from Burning*. Boston: South End Press, 2007, p. 204.

28. Ibid., p. 206.

29. Charles Derber, *Greed to Green*. New York: Routledge, 2010.

30. Ibid.

31. "Warning: College Students, This Editorial May Upset You," *LA Times Editorial Board*, Mar. 31, 2014.

32. Edward Helmore, "Minnie Driver: Men Like Matt Damon 'Cannot Understand What Abuse Is like,'" *The Guardian*, Dec. 17, 2017, theguardian.com.

33. Ibid.
34. Batya Ungar-Sargon, *'Affirmative Consent' Is Bad for Women*. New York: New Republic, Sep. 16, 2014.
35. Cathy Young, "Campus Rape: The Problem With 'Yes Means Yes,'" *New York Times Magazine*, Aug. 29, 2014.
36. Peter Beinart, "A Violent Attack on Free Speech at Middlebury," *The Atlantic*, Mar. 6, 2017, Washington, DC.

Chapter 6

1. Charles Derber, *Welcome to the Revolution*. New York: Routledge, 2017, p. 4.
2. Thomas Piketty, *Capital in the Twenty-First Century*. Cambridge, MA: Harvard University Press, 2017.
3. Jeremy Rifkin, *The European Dream*. New York: Tarcher/Penguin, 2004, pp. 212–13.
4. Ibid., p. 212.
5. George Lakey, *Viking Economics*, Reprint edition. Brooklyn, N.Y.: Melville House, 2017.
6. Charles Derber, "Capitalism: Big Surprises in Recent Polls," *People's World*, May 24, 2010.
7. Rev. William Barber, cited in Julia Craven, "2 Ministers are Trying to Revive the Campaign to End Poverty that MLK Started," *Huffpost*, Apr. 9, 2018, huffingtonpost.com.
8. Ibid.
9. Ibid.
10. Adam Gabbatt and Mike Elk, "Teachers Strikes: Meet the Leaders of the Movement Marching Across America," *The Guardian*, Apr. 16, 2018, theguardian.com.
11. Ibid.
12. Nicole M. Aschoff, "Feminism Against Capitalism," *Jacobin*, Feb. 29, 2016, jacobinmag.com.
13. Susan Faludi, cited in Aschoff, ibid.
14. NOW, "Economic Justice," now.org.
15. National Nurses United, "About National Nurses United," nationalnursesunited.org.
16. Moveon.org, "A Short History of MoveOn," front.moveon.org.
17. Bernie Sanders, cited in Derber, *Welcome to the Revolution*, p. 211.
18. Nina Turner, "An Interview with Nina Turner," *Jacobin*, June 15, 2018, jacobinmag.org.
19. Sarah Jones, "Minutes: News and Notes," *The New Republic*, June 26, 2018, newrepublc.com.
20. Kevin Rose, "Meet the Seattle Socialist Leading the Fight for a Minimum $15 Wage," *New York Magazine*, May 26, 2014, nymag.com.
21. Ibid.
22. Gar Alperovitz, "The Cooperative Economy: A Conversation With Gar Alperovitz," May and July editions of *Orion Magazine*, 2014, garalperovitz.com.
23. Ibid.
24. "Massachusetts 2018 Ballot Measures," Ballotpedia, ballotpedia.org.
25. Thomas Piketty, *Capital in the Twenty-First Century*, p. 515.
26. Ibid., p. 495.
27. Sean McElwee, "Millennials are Significantly More Progressive than Their Parents," *The Washington Post*, Mar. 24, 2016.
28. Ibid.

29. Ibid.
30. Ibid.
31. "Subsidiarity: The Role of Government," devp.org.
32. United Nations, "Declaration of Human Rights," un.org.
33. Ibid.
34. Jeremy Rifkin, *The European Dream*, p. 273.
35. Ibid.

INDEX

Entries in **bold** refer to tables.